OLEJURU LANFEAR

The Fundamentals Of Planning

Understanding merchandise planning for retail success

First edition

ISBN: 978-0-6487256-0-2

Cover art by Olejuru Lanfear
Illustration by Hannah Brown

This book was professionally typeset on Reedsy.
Find out more at reedsy.com

Dedicated to my family

Contents

Preface   ii
UNDERSTANDING MERCHANDISE PLANNING   1
AN OVERVIEW OF MERCHANDISE PLANNING   7
PLANNING DEPARTMENT STRUCTURE   20
LET'S DEFINE MERCHANDISE PLANNING   30
WHAT DOES MERCHANDISE PLAN-
NING DO?   38
HOW DOES PLANNING DO WHAT IT DOES?   48
NO PLANNING? NO PROBLEM   58
PLANNING: ART OR SCIENCE?   70
TECHNOLOGY IN RETAIL: YESTERDAY,
TODAY AND TOMORROW   74
A BRIEF HISTORY OF RETAILING: 1700 ONWARDS   88
WHAT DOES IT TAKE TO BECOME A PLANNER?   104
ABOUT ME   115
ABOUT SLOPPYSUCCESS   122
SLOPPYSCLASSES   123
MASTERING A NEW SKILL   133
GLOSSARY   136

Preface

Before you spend any time reading this book, I would like to let you know what this book isn't. This book is most definitely not a how-to guide of any sort; nor is it a book that will give you a list of formulas for calculating key performance indicators, gross margin, how much stock to buy or anything else. If that is something you are looking for, your time would be better served watching my online classes that cover these topics.

This book is for those who are interested in a behind-the-scenes view of merchandise planning. One reason for this could be because you deal with people involved in merchandise planning and want to gain a better understanding of the role and how it fits into an organisation.

Also in this book is a quick peek into the retail industry in general, from how it was, to how it is now and how it could be in the future.

My hope is that you'll learn about merchandise planning and come to see it as an integral part of any retail organisation, regardless of size.

UNDERSTANDING MERCHANDISE PLANNING

Keepers of the purse.
As people who hold the purse strings in a buying department, the
role of a merchandise planner is not one that is truly understood by
people within retail. The function itself is also misunderstood
within the wider retail environ.

Merchandise planning — also known as trade planning, planning or merchandising — should not be confused with the other merchandising role, i.e. visual merchandising. Merchandise planning is a function that usually sits within a buying department, although sometimes it sits under finance.

Those who perform the role can be thought of as the 'accountant for the buying department', as merchandise planners are the ones who hold the purse strings when it comes to how much to spend on new products, replenishing products, discounting products and when to spend on these things.

Operating mainly behind the scenes, it is not as glamorous as the buying function, but still remains an essential part of any retail organisation.

Just like the exchange of goods and services between people has always occurred, there has also always been the function of planning. It is a function driven by need. As long as there is a need and there are people willing to fulfil that need, the planning function will always be around in one form or another. Thus, it is a function that will continue to evolve and adapt, much like the retail industry.

This in effect means the demand and supply of goods and services is here to stay as people will always need to buy, produce, find or make things to sell. The industry will take on different forms over time and people will be able to satisfy their desire to purchase in a variety of ways, as can be seen by the array of options available to purchase and receive goods and services today.

In the middle of the 20th Century, goods and services were purchased by going door to door. Milk, eggs and cheese could be bought at your front door.

The door-to-door selling method gave way to general stores, which then gave way to supermarkets, where people went to purchase milk, eggs, cheese and other food items. Supermarkets evolved and now you can order your goods online and have them delivered to your home or pick up your order in-store. This example shows that the only thing that has changed is how we purchase eggs, milk and cheese and not whether we need to buy eggs, milk and cheese.

Let's look at it in a different way.

The exchange of goods and services has evolved through the years; from bartering with friends, neighbours and anyone who has what you need, peddlers calling on you to sell their wares and selling goods at markets, to early brick and mortar stores, which usually took the form of a general store where you could purchase most things. By the mid 20th century, the party plan model became popular thanks to companies like Tupperware. Tupperware consultants found people who were willing to invite their friends and family to their homes to be introduced to and buy products. In the 21st century, 'pure play' online stores (eCommerce) started appearing and now we can sell using specific apps via smart phones (mCommerce) and sell on social platforms (sCommerce).

Being able to use these methods to get your products in front of customers has created a multi-channel environment, which has changed the retailing industry. Even the least technologically-advanced customer has an expectation that they can buy things from multiple channels.

All these different ways of being able to get products to customers doesn't mean more sales for businesses. If anything, it means an increase in costs, at least in the short term, as new skills need to be learnt and taught in order to meet customers' expectations. As the quantity in units sold isn't increasing exponentially, there is no need to drastically increase the amount spent on purchases. What is needed is planning.

Planning involves deciding where to place what has been bought so orders can be met seamlessly, without sales suffering, while profit levels are maintained. *Who is best placed to make these plans?* That is the million dollar question. It isn't just the buyer; it isn't just the logistics department; it isn't just the planning department; it isn't just the accounting department; it isn't just the store staff. It is a combination of these departments and all the other departments within a retail business.

None of these departments work in isolation. They all feed into each other and, more importantly, one department they feed into is the merchandise planning department.

The planning department is a central point in any business that deals with buying and selling products at the same time. The planning department is the first line in making a retail business profitable, which it does by constantly watching sales performance.

Product costs, selling prices, volume of inventory to meet sales, volume of unproductive inventory, how much profit is made per item sold and how much profit is made for all items sold are some of the information the planning department stays on top of at all times.

After the planning department performs its tasks, the information is passed onto other parts of the business, who then do what they do. The accounts department uses the information to create the business balance sheet and profit and loss accounts. Expenses are paid and what is left over is reinvested in the business, paid out as dividends or invested in other businesses.

Time to ask the million dollar question slightly differently again. Does this mean merchandise planning will always be needed?

That is a tricky question to answer. As a standalone department, possibly not. As a function within a retail business, 'Yes!', as there will always be a need for some sort of merchandise planning function.

This answer is based on people always needing things and our willingness to trade with others to get what we need or want. Traders will always need to make sure they have enough inventory to satisfy demand and make a profit for their efforts.

Not all businesses will be able to afford a merchandise planning department, which is why there are hybrid roles combining buying with a bit of planning. In theory, there is nothing wrong with doing this and it works well for a lot of retailers.

That said, there are pertinent questions to ask about opting to have hybrid roles within a retail business, such as, can the person performing the role:

- Be good at both selecting products and analysing performance throughout the season and afterwards?
- Make timely pricing decisions, ensuring margin is maintained?
- Constantly check inventory is sitting in the right locations and that the right locations have inventory?
- Manage all the relationships needed to perform the role?

Or does this hybrid role only really focus on the pre-season elements of getting a product and not in-season and post-season management? Also, would the hybrid role be skewed more towards buying or planning?

AN OVERVIEW OF
MERCHANDISE PLANNING

If it can be measured, it can be improved.
A standalone function within a buying department, merchandise
planning focuses on measuring and improving performance.

Planning is not a well known business function. Having worked in the retailing industry since the age of 14, it wasn't until I was in my second year at university, where I studied Marketing, Retailing and Distribution, that I came across merchandise planning and even then, I didn't fully understand that it was a standalone role. I thought it was something done by buyers, as they are the ones who purchase products.

A Career Path To Merchandise Planning

Like all roles within an organisation, there are different paths to follow in order to become a planner.

One such path is to start off as an allocator. Even though the allocation of inventory usually sits under the merchandise planning umbrella, it is a specialist function that can stand on its own.

Allocators are the ones who maintain stock levels in stores. They chase suppliers for when stock deliveries will arrive in the warehouse and they liaise with suppliers to come up with delivery schedules that prevent stock from sitting in either the supplier or retailer's warehouse for too long.

If the retailer has inventory delivered directly from the supplier to stores, allocators provide the supplier with each store's allocation quantity, monitor delivery accuracy and ensure they are delivered on time and in the right quantities. Overall, they are the ones who keep a very close eye on inventory to make sure at the end of the season, there is no inventory left to sell.

When I first started down the path to becoming a merchandise planner, I remember being told by a colleague that the way to measure the true performance of an allocator was if they were able to finish the season with no stock left to call upon at the supplier and also no stock left in stores. In other words, having no old season inventory lingering when the new season starts.

Allocation ensures the right products get to the right stores, at the right time and in the right quantities.

Like other retail roles, the role of an allocator has evolved into demand planning. Demand planning is not just about keeping stores stocked, it is also about predicting the amount of inventory that would be needed to fulfil demand.

Allocators may be called different things in different organisations and the role has grown. With the increased use of technology to determine how much stock each store is to get, the role has evolved to include the creation of reports that shows inventory performance. These reports are used to determine product performance improvement opportunities that will result in customers getting the product they want, when they want it, using their preferred shopping channel.

Defining what an allocator does is easy. Telling people you send stock to stores is simple enough or even if you say you 'allocate' stock to stores, people get it. An allocator's role is clear.

Having navigated my way to becoming a merchandise planner from the bottom up, I knew what merchandise planning was about. I also thought, perhaps naively, others knew what the role was about.

There was one thing that started to indicate planning wasn't a well known role or function and that was, whenever asked what I did for a living, people's faces had a blank look when I said I was a merchandise planner. Even changing the title from merchandise planner to planner didn't help, as essentially, people asked if I was a town planner or a financial planner.

Not only did the job title produce a blank look on faces, understanding what the role was about also generated the same blank look, with a little bit of confusion thrown into the mix.

Merchandise planning is a function that naturally lends itself to easily integrate into other areas of a business. To truly understand planning, you have to think of it not as a standalone function, but one that has to work simultaneously and in harmony with multiple parts of a business.

Buyers and planners work closely together and can be thought of as two sides of the same coin. In a good buyer/planner relationship, it would not be unexpected for management to question whether there is a need to have both roles. This is sometimes the view within organisations that do not understand the value merchandise planning brings to an organisation or ones that think planning is just a department that produces reports.

As a standalone department, merchandise planning has access to a lot of data and it is part of the department's role to make sense of that data. This is why whenever it comes to creating reports, planners usually have a very big say in how they are created.

During sales blackout periods, when sales figures are kept private rather than made public, those within planning still have access to all sales data because they are needed to create reports used by management. These reports are created and circulated to different levels within the business.

So, the perception of planning in a business is that they deal with inventory, create reports, play with numbers and ask lots of questions.

Actually, 'playing with numbers all day' was how I explained what I did for a living to my children when they were younger and I sometimes use this explanation with grown ups, too.

So, what is the purpose of planning and what is the point of having a planning department?

One thing that planning does is it brings different areas of a business together and provides early performance visibility.

Working closely with buyers, the warehouse, marketing, IT and finance, planners often collaborate with their appointed counterparts in these areas so they can serve their customers better.

The customers in question are not consumers, but those who sell to consumers. In other words, whomever holds inventory to sell onto consumers are the merchandise planning department's customers. So for brick and mortar retailers that would be the stores; for online retailers that hold inventory, it would be the warehouse. For online retailers that do not hold inventory, a planner's customer would be where the inventory is shipped from, i.e. the suppliers. This makes for an interesting relationship between suppliers and planners, as they are each other's customers.

The reason these customers should be put first — instead of members of the public — has to do with ensuring the availability of stock to sell to consumers. After all, if there's no inventory to sell, there would be no sales. No sales means no profit and no profit means the business would not be able to remain viable.

Ultimately, the function of planning is to work with other parts of a business to ensure their customers have the goods they need so that they can sell them as quickly and profitably as possible.

Versatility Of Merchandise Planning

Merchandise planning is a versatile role, in that it is easy to move from one type of retailer to another; for instance, a planner can switch from working in fashion to working in hardgoods. The type of products may be different. Some of the differences between fashion and hardgoods are sizing, the level of repeat purchases and how quickly and often new styles are introduced. Even with these differences, a planner can switch relatively easily between these product types.

This ability to switch product areas is made easier for planners by knowing the key information to look for in reports, having become well versed in looking at and creating many different reports over time. Creating and analysing multiple reports leads to knowing which numbers need to be called out and what they mean in relation to the health of the product area the planner is responsible for. Also, speaking to others in the buying department to get a better understanding of the department helps make the switch seamless.

So, it is the personal preference of the merchandise planner that determines if they stick with one industry type or not. There are planners who prefer the fashion industry, those who prefer general retailers and those who prefer digital products. Some planners like to get a wide range of experience by working with different product types and selling channels, e.g. direct selling, subscription based retailers, online (pure play) retailers, etc.

There is nothing wrong with sticking with a specific product type or channel as a planner, especially as each product area and channel has its own idiosyncrasies. For instance, as fashion is highly seasonal, if a particular colour introduced for that season isn't sold within a specific period of time, trying to sell it a couple of years later is much harder as the item is no longer relevant. This is why keeping an eye on how quickly products sell, by using sell through and rate of sale calculations, is important in preventing the purchase of too much inventory in the first place.

Being on top of sell throughs is not as critical when planning hardgoods as the fashion trends in hardgoods tend to have a much longer lifecycle. A set of pliers with this year's Pantone™ colour of the year can still be sold next year without having to mark it down.

More critical in hardgoods is to keep a close eye on inventory levels, as the rate of sale is lower. This could easily lead to having an excess amount of inventory on hand as more products are purchased without getting out of the inventory currently being sat on.

Generally I would say it is a good idea for planners to get experience in different product areas as each area's idiosyncrasies adds to a planner's list of skills. This is particularly true when it comes to dealing with head-scratching planning situations.

Working in a general retailer with multiple selling channels is one way to get exposure to different product types. Doing this is also a low risk way for planners to decide if they want to be a general merchandise planner or specialist merchandise planner.

Creating Budgets

When it comes to budgeting, planners come up with a budget using the 'bottom up' method, while senior management and the board come up with high level budget figures using a 'top down' approach. Ideally, these numbers would be the same. In reality, they usually aren't.

The first set of budgeting numbers the planning department comes up with is based on current performance. A percentage increase or decrease is overlaid onto this, based on what is predicted to happen during the period the budget is being prepared for.

The budget figures that planning comes up with are critical in knowing if the business plans are on track to succeed. As the planner makes note of how much money is coming into the business at a granular level, planners tend to get an early indication of the feasibility of budgets being achieved. Planners are also in a unique position of knowing how healthy the business is based on results seen from monitoring actual revenue performance against planned performance.

Think of it this way: Planning records the total amount of

money brought in from general sales and keeps track of how much gross margin is created, as well as how much inventory was used to generate sales and gross margin. Planning then predicts how much money will come into a business by creating a sales budget. This budget is in turn used to determine if the expense budgets created by other departments are affordable.

Maybe this is why planners are a bit like accountants.

Planners and accountants have similar traits when it comes to planning. We are happy to spend if we can afford it and if the amount spent brings in additional sales and margin while reducing inventory.

The main difference I have seen between planners who were formerly accountants and non-accountant planners is that non-accountant planners are more willing to take calculated risks on products. These risks tend to be taken in a very controlled way. The spend for these risks come out of what I like to call the 'balancing money' bucket. Each planner who has control over how much can be spent on inventory should always have a 'balancing money' bucket.

The 'balancing money' bucket is where product trials can start. It can be used to fund special buys to see if they are viable options as a replacement or addition to the current product range. They can also be used in a not so fun way to cover minor purchasing overspends.

Planners do have to be confident there will be a positive return on purchases made with this bucket of money.

Improving Plans

'If it can be measured, it can be improved.'

This is a motto all planning departments should live by. This also nicely explains how planners ensure the books remain balanced.

All reports created need to be measured against something to give the figures meaning. Sales, inventory and margin are measured against budget, forecast, last year, last week, year to date, month to date and any other comparisons one can think of.

Assumptions, conclusions and plans are derived from these reports with the aim of improving whichever metric is being looked at. For instance, if there is too much inventory being held in relation to the amount of sales being achieved, action can be taken to get those two metrics in line with each other. Plans can be put in place to either increase sales through the use of promotions and markdowns or reduce inventory levels by negotiating with suppliers and having them take some back.

Suppliers may be willing to take stock back so long as they are able to resell the inventory or you take something else in its place. Using this method to reduce inventory requires there to be a win/win outcome for both parties.

PLANNING DEPARTMENT STRUCTURE

Where does it sit?
Wherever the function sits in an organisation, planning needs its own systems, people, processes and a way to extract data. These four things are what's needed in all planning departments, regardless of the structure of where the department sits in a retailer's hierarchy.

Each merchandise planning department you come across is different and that is because it depends on the needs of the business. In some organisations, planning sits within the buying department; in others, it sits within finance.

A classic planning department looks something like this:

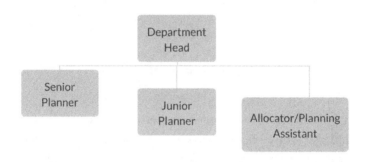

Flat department structure

This is a flat structure as each role reports directly into the department head. An alternative structure could be:

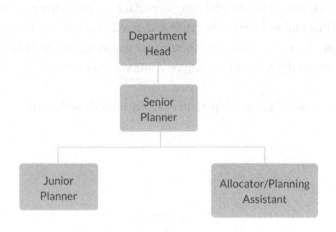

Vertical department structure

In both structures, starting as an allocator can lead to becoming a merchandise planner, even though stock allocation has its own career path, where allocators take on more product area of responsibility and team management.

For a merchandise planning department to be operational, here is what is needed:

Data - Sales data, inventory data and purchasing data are three data types needed. The data is used to create reports, so a summary of performance is available for all to see.

Systems - Some sort of system is needed to store all the data. The system needs to have the ability to store historical and current data at the lowest level. Ideally, the system would also be able to handle future plans as well, such as planned purchases, budgeted and forecasted sales and inventory. Most organisations I have come across use Excel for budgeting and forecasting sales, instead of an actual planning system.

People - Even though there is a lot of reliance on systems, there is still a need for the human element. People are needed to decide what goes into reports, who gets the reports, frequency of report distribution, analyse information in the report and come up with recommendations from information on the reports.

Process - Even with data, systems and people, having a process to follow is essential in a planning department. This isn't done for the sake of having a process, it is needed so the planning department is in sync with other departments in the business.

For instance, there is no point having a sales meeting on a Wednesday if the business week starts on a Sunday or Monday. By Wednesday, last week's data is too old for managers to make any meaningful or actionable decisions that would affect the current week's performance, as three days of trading has taken place.

In broad terms, these are the four things needed to get a merchandise planning department set up and operational.

There are specific systems that can be purchased to help set up processes and collect and store detailed data. This tends to be the route a lot of larger retailers go down. However, a lot of smaller retailers may not have enough funds to purchase planning systems as it may not be financially justifiable based on turnover. Thankfully, spreadsheets are a powerful business tool and a template can be created and used in lieu of purchasing a specific planning system.

The great thing about using spreadsheets is that sheets can be linked with each other. If opting to use Google Sheets rather than Excel, add ons can be bolted on to fully integrate all sheets and provide a complete picture.

The Merchandise Planning Role

Merchandise planning is a simple function, even though it is sometimes made more complicated than it needs to be. The formulas used to analyse the relationship between sales, stock and margin can be daunting, which is why this book purposefully doesn't contain any formulas.

Plus, with the age we live in, you can get performance calculations freely on the Internet. As mentioned earlier, this book is about what planning is, how planning as a function fits into a business and how it works. The repetition of certain concepts has been to either reinforce a point or because it explains a point being made.

Having a merchandise planning department is not just about report running or report creation. If this is what you think planning is, then chances are your business is wasting its money on salaries.

Added to this, chances are there would also be a high turnover of staff, as hiring someone to be a planner and then have them only create and run reports leads to the planner becoming demotivated. Plus, if this is all they do, there would be little to no time left for the planner to critically look at reports to come up with recommendations on how to improve performance.

One way to overcome this is to actually get someone whose sole job is to either work alongside or be part of the planning department and create all core reports for the business. They can create and publish weekly reports, create forecast accuracy reports, range review templates and any other planning documents and templates to be used company wide.

I have seen this work quite successfully when I worked for one of the largest retailers in the world, who at the time I worked there did not have a reporting system and used Excel for reporting.

In some organisations, it is the IT department that is charged with creating reports. From observation and experience, this only works well if there is someone from the planning department who works alongside the IT department and they are both willing to find acceptable solutions whenever there is an issue to overcome.

A third option is to have the accounts department create and distribute reports. I have a vague recollection of an organisation I worked for early on in my career doing this. The reports created were at a high level and weren't really at the level of detail needed by buyers. So, even though the reports were great at giving information after the fact, the reports didn't compare what was happening now to what had happened in the past or what will happen in the future.

For small retailers, in other words those who do not have the budget for a planning department, one solution worth investigating is to use their accountants as a pseudo planning department. The thinking behind this is based on the fact that accountants already gather information on a regular basis for sales revenue and inventory when preparing balance sheets. So, with some tweaking of the balance sheet report, it could be possible for an accountant that specialises in retail to create meaningful reports that would benefit small retailers.

A possible downside to doing this would be the infrequency of the reports. The reports would really need to be created and published in a way that allows timely decisions to be made. If this can be done, then using an accountant could be a viable option.

Hierarchy Helps Planners

Merchandise planning skills are transferable from retailer to retailer. This transfer is made much easier when there is a clear product hierarchy within a retailer. As the product hierarchy groups like products together, the switch from an own brand retailer to a branded retailer becomes seamless as brand is one of the levels in the product hierarchy.

It's a similar case when going from a retailer with only brick and mortar stores to one that sells only online. Rather than looking at store performance, planners will look at performance by geographical location instead.

There is no need to make it more complicated than this.

Key Performance Indicators

It is a misconception people have about planning that the most important key performance indicator is sales. Don't get me wrong, sales are important and the more sales revenue produced, the better. It is just not the be all and end all.

More important than sales is profit. Added to that, having good cash flow is what will keep a business going regardless of the trading environment.

Sales won't come about, nor will profit or cash flow, if there is nothing to sell. This means inventory is also a performance indicator to keep a close eye on.

With each of these individual indicators being important, planners tend to look at the relationship between them in order to determine where performance issues lie.

Planners look at the relationship between sales and inventory and the relationship between sales and cost.

The relationship between sales and inventory shows how long inventory would last for based on current and future sales levels. The relationship between product sales and product cost shows how profitable the products being sold are.

The margin calculated, based on a single unit's cost price and full retail price is called the 'first margin'. It is called the first margin as it is the first of many margin calculations done.

The margin realised in a buying department is the gross margin. The gross margin doesn't have any operating costs deducted from it. That is something that is done by the accounting department.

The gross margin is simply how much is left after the products' supplier gets paid, once the product is sold. This could also be called the 'reported margin'.

The reported margin shared with others has usually had all selling price reductions taken into account. Therefore, the first margin is more often than not different to the reported gross margin.

Other than selling price reductions such as markdowns during sale time, on the spot discounts given to customers or discounts as a result of promotions on offer, there are also cost price reductions that affect the final margin seen.

These cost price reductions could be as a result of terms negotiated with suppliers and are included in supplier contracts. An example of a change in cost price could be in the form of rebates. For instance, there could be a rebate offered reducing the cost value of inventory over a certain 'age' in lieu of sending inventory back to the supplier. The cost price rebate could be one of the clauses listed in the supplier contract.

The effect on gross margin as a result of selling price and cost price reductions is that selling price reductions are visible for all to see immediately, whereas cost price reductions need to be calculated at the end of a specified period, e.g. month, quarter or year.

LET'S DEFINE MERCHANDISE PLANNING

So, what do you do?
Ask five different planners this question and you'll get five different
answers. Read this chapter to get a succinct answer to the question.

There are different definitions of merchandise planning. Each merchandise planner you ask would give their own definition of what planning is. Definitions are usually based on how people see planning fit into an organisation, how they themselves became planners and the definition given may also be based on key responsibilities of a planning role.

The most common definition of planning uses the Five (5) Rights.

Planning is defined as: *'Getting the right products to the right stores, at the right time, for the right price and in the right quantities'.*

As far as definitions go, this one seems simple enough. However it doesn't really justify having a specific department to do this as each of the 'rights' can be performed by non planners.

Right product - The buyer is the one to select and decide which products to buy.

Right stores - Store managers can determine if a product is right for their store or not, based on knowledge of their store's demographics.

Right time - The buyer has selected a product for a specific sales period and the inventory is sent to stores via the warehouse.

Right price - When the buyer selects a product to buy, the cost price and the margin to achieve is used to come up with a selling price, alongside knowing what competitors are charging for the same or similar products and what customers are willing to pay. That is to say, the market determines the price.

Right quantities - Similar to *'right stores'*, those who are actually going to be selling the product, e.g. the store manager, can determine the quantities they need to sell.

Based on the *'5 Rights'* definition of planning, merchandise planning is a function that can be done by other parts of a business. Plus, it sounds more like a just-in-time definition, which can be attributed to the supply chain function rather than the planning function.

An observation with this definition of planning: There is no mention of how the *'5 Rights'* work together. This definition leads me to conclude that each area works in isolation and independently of each other, which isn't the case.

Let's look at another definition. On John Hobson's website[1], which has been my go to site for all things planning related, merchandise planning is defined as:

'...a systematic approach. It is aimed at maximising return on investment, through planning sales and inventory in order to increase profitability. It does this by maximising sales potential and minimising losses from markdowns and stockouts, while taking into account the constraints of a retail business.'

That is a comprehensive definition of what planning does. However, to someone who isn't a merchandise planner and

---

[1]   **http://www.planfact.co.uk/what-is-merchandise-planning**

is trying to figure out what planning is and what merchandise planners do, it still doesn't give a simple definition.

Don't get me wrong, the definition is great and it sums up planning perfectly. It just doesn't provide a simple enough definition for a layperson to understand.

Look at it this way. Picture being in a crowded room with lots of conversations going on at the same time, music playing in the background and sounds from outside coming into the room each time a door is open and closed. This type of environment makes hearing what others are saying a challenge, which is why conversations are usually kept light and entertaining. In that environment, if someone asks you what merchandise planning is, would you really use either of these definitions?

To a layperson and by that I mean anyone who isn't a merchandise planner, would either of these definitions make sense? Probably not.

It took me years to distil what planning is into a succinct phrase that is easy to remember, takes less than 10 seconds to say and answers the question 'what is merchandise planning?' and 'what do you do for work?' at the same time. It is a definition with potential.

The answer I give is by no means as comprehensive as the systematic approach definition mentioned earlier. What it does do is give a concise and understandable explanation, which can be further delved into if more information is needed or more questions asked.

Here's how I define merchandise planning as well as what a merchandise planner does.

Question: What is merchandise planning?

Answer: Merchandise planning *'ensures sales, stock and margin are aligned with plans'.*

Question: What does a merchandise planner do?

Answer: A merchandise planner *'ensures sales, stock and margin are aligned with plans'.*

Yes, both answers are the same.

This definition can be played with, by changing the word *'aligned'* to *'inline'* and the word *'plans'* to *'budget'.*

This definition uses the *keep it simple, stupid* method. It gets straight to the point and mentions the three main areas planning and planners are involved in.

The same phrase can be tweaked a little to define what merchandise planning is and what a merchandise planner does. You could say, merchandise planners ensure:

- Sales, stock and margin are inline with each other
- Sales, stock and margin are balanced
- Sales, stock and margin are aligned.

A further question that could be asked is, if these definition variations are used: Is ...aligned to what? That is a simple question to answer. Sales, stock and margin needs to be aligned to the budget.

This definition is a great one to use when talking to people who want to know what planning is and what planners do. At this level of conversation there is no need to mention markdowns, out of stocks or methods used to make sure the desired return on investment is achieved. It's what I like to call a social setting definition.

Another simple way to define planning using the same simplistic method is to say merchandise planning and merchandise planners 'ensure retailers make as much money as possible off of as little inventory as possible and as few markdowns as possible.'

This definition makes sense to use when talking to those who understand what goes into making a profit. It's not so useful to use if speaking to a visual or creative person.

Just like when filling in a form that asks what your job title is and there isn't enough space given to write 'merchandise planner' and the job title is abbreviated to 'planner', which can get confused with financial or town planner, the best way to tell people what a merchandise planner is and does is by distilling the answer into the least number of words possible.

WHAT DOES MERCHANDISE PLANNING DO?

More than report creation...
This chapter takes a closer look at a comprehensive definition of merchandise planning, which encompasses all areas of the planning function.

Now we know what planning is and what a planner does, how do planners go about aligning sales, stock and margin?

This question tends to be asked by those who are truly interested in knowing more about merchandise planning, rather than those who are just making conversation.

Even though saying I make sure sales, stock and margin are aligned with plans is usually enough to give people a sense of what I do, I don't believe they truly understand everything I am saying. I know this because I sometimes change the work 'stock' and 'margin' to 'inventory' and 'profit,' and still get the same baffled expression or confusion on what merchandise planning is.

If I notice they still aren't clear, I use my extended pitch, which goes something like this.

'When you walk into a store and see all those items that have been marked down, it is the planner that identifies what to markdown, when to mark it down and how much to mark it down by, without the retailer losing money.'

This provides enough of a general explanation to give an idea of what some aspects of planning is about. Obviously, planning is about so much more than marking items down.

What I like about all the definitions and explanations given is that the three broad areas of sales, stock and margin are mentioned. It also highlights a planner's primary focus is on the alignment of these areas and by its omission, the product area looked after by the planner is secondary.

The explanation given of what a planner does, i.e. *'ensures sales, stock and margin are aligned and inline with plans'* refers to how to explain what a merchandise planner does in polite conversation. It also suffices as an explanation in a social setting where there are invariably lots of conversations happening at the same time. Hence, the short answer.

To give a more involved answer to the question *'what is merchandise planning?,'* the best answer I have come across that encapsulates all aspects of planning is the one given by John Hobson of www.planfact.co.uk.[2]

He says: 'Merchandise planning is *a systematic approach. It is aimed at maximising return on investment, through planning sales and inventory in order to increase profitability. It does this by maximising sales potential and minimising losses from markdowns and stockouts, while taking into account the constraints of a retail business'.*

This definition gives a nice simple explanation to anyone who wants to understand planning as a function. Let's break the definition down and I'll give my interpretation of what it means.

Systematic Approach

There is a base method that has to be used in all planning departments. For instance, when creating a budget, some form

---

[2] **http://www.planfact.co.uk/what-is-merchandise-planning**

of data is needed to base any future budgets on. That data needs to be obtained from somewhere, by someone.

Confused?

To come up with a budget, a specific set of historical data is needed. This data is housed in a particular order, in a specific place. Extracting the data is done systematically, e.g. current year, last year and the year before that.

Maximising Return On Investment

This one is pretty straightforward and self explanatory. Simply put it means, get as much sales and profit as possible off of as little inventory as possible.

Getting as many sales as possible refers to having people repeatedly purchase what you have to sell at the price you are selling it for. This is to be done without over committing on any inventory or under committing, come to think of it. Making stock 'sweat' is the key here; worded differently: Get as much profit as possible from the least amount of stock possible.

Logically, a brick and mortar store's stockholding would need to be higher than an online retailer with no physical stores. As a result of this need, physical stores have to carry stock for display purposes, safety stock, ordering cycle and order lag time. Pure online retailers do not need to carry stock for display, since images and product descriptions are used to showcase a product.

Other areas you'll also want to maximise your return on investment are: systems, people and time.

These areas are not usually included when referring to maximising return on investment. Like inventory, however, a planner should also ensure that the return on investment in these areas are maximised by getting the right data, speaking to the right people and using time wisely. There is no point spending three weeks coming up with a list of markdowns using data that has been collated using only one metric e.g. sales, only to find the optimum markdown start date has passed.

Planning Sales And Inventory

A character on a popular TV show on the BBC, for those who are familiar with UK TV, Mark Fowler in *Eastenders*, was asked by his sister Michelle, who was a mature university student, '*What is history?*' His answer was quite simple and accurate: '*...history is a record of the past and a guide to the future.*' That definition also sums up what the 'planning' part of 'merchandise planning' is about.

In order for sales and inventory to be planned, we need to know what has happened in the past in order to create a future sales and inventory plan. If historical information that directly relates to a product area being planned is not available, as is the case for a new product, historical information from a closely related source can be used to create a sales and inventory plan.

Increase Profitability

Profitability is also known as margin. In planning, we look at the overall gross margin rate first. Then we drill down to see what is contributing to the margin rate and what the rate translates to in margin value.

In my time in planning, I have found the margin rate to be a more accurate indication of overall profitability, as it looks at the relative performance between sales and profit, allowing for a more accurate indication of what the margin value is going to be. Using margin rate is also a better long term indication of what profit value to expect.

Markdowns And Stock Outs

There is nothing wrong with planned markdowns, as the effect on margin has been factored into budgets and forecasts. It is the unplanned markdowns that creates issues. A single unplanned markdown has the potential to wipe away profits that have been achieved.

As for when an item is out of stock, i.e. stock outs, it creates a situation where there are missed sales. Missed sales leads to reduced profits and unless stock outs are managed by ensuring stock commitments are adjusted accordingly, there is the possibility of becoming overstocked, which leads to having to markdown the product more than initially planned in order to get rid of excess inventory and free up some cash.

That explains rather simply what planning does. John Hobson

at planfact.co.uk has a post on his site that is worthwhile reading. It can be found at http://planfact.co.uk/what-is-merchandise-planning.

From Vision To Strategy

There is an overall vision a merchandise planning department has, which is an offshoot of the company's overarching vision. That vision is translated into a strategy that looks at the different ways the vision can be achieved. merchandise planning will have a part to play in the overall strategy.

Merchandise planning is about developing ways to enable a company to sell a range of products that delivers sales and profit targets. A merchandiser planner will work closely with a buyer to ensure the product that's bought will enable them to achieve this.

A merchandise planner will also work with supply chain and logistics to ensure products come into the business and is sent onto stores in a timely manner. As it is the objective of the merchandise planning management team to get the correct balance between the product expectations of the customer and the objectives of the company's financial strategy.

When Do Planners Get Involved?

Having planners involved from the very beginning of the buying process is ideal. This involvement in pre-season planning gives planners more confidence when coming up with plans, as the buyer's thoughts about how they see the product selling can be incorporated.

Pre-season planning for planners usually starts before budgets have been created for the upcoming season. Reason being, lead times for products don't necessarily fit into buying cycles and suppliers need to have figures available so they are better placed to ensure stock is delivered on time. It also means suppliers can give more accurate costs when they are given purchase quantities.

Report Creation

When planners are working on something new, reports are pulled off the system. The more complicated the task, the more data is needed. Once all relevant data has been pulled off, it is then looked at in a variety of ways. This is done so conclusions can be reached and theories put into practice.

Data and the analysis of data for a specific purpose, is a planner's friend. For pre-season planning, planners look quantitatively at data to answer questions like: What worked, what didn't work, when should new lines be introduced and so on. For instance, a category may have generated even more sales and margin if there was a consistent supply of stock throughout the season, rather than a large chunk of inventory coming in one go.

Ad hoc report creation is an inevitable part of planning. Outside of creating ad hoc reports, there are, thankfully, standard reports that provide the majority of information required to look at performance and make decisions.

With that said, if there are too many ad hoc reports being created, it shows one of two things. It either shows the standard reports are inadequate or it shows the standard reports are adequate but need to be tweaked a little to answer more in depth questions being asked.

Whether you have a standard suite of reports or are constantly creating ad hoc reports, be aware the more time spent creating reports, the less time will be available to analyse the information to come up with recommendations and action plans.

This also raises another question of who should create reports. Should there be a sole person in the planning department whose job would be to create all standard and ad hoc reports?

If there is a single person creating and maintaining all reports, the first question to ask would be: Is there enough work for the role to be a full time one? Then the next question would be: Would it be quicker for planners to create their own ad hoc reports as they know what it is they are looking for in the data?

The reason it is a good idea to have a report creation process is because planners need to be able to translate information into budgets, forecasts and plans, with contingencies if criterion like sell through rates are not met. As there are always deadlines to meet, there needs to be enough time to analyse the data.

Just like when we were in school and had to edit our writing, there needs to be sufficient time between finishing and editing in order to be able to spot errors easily. With report creation, a similar gap in time is needed between a report being created and the information being analysed.

Doing this also means the likelihood of being able to spot things that require further investigation or that may raise questions later. This leads to answers being found for these issues before the questions are asked.

HOW DOES PLANNING DO WHAT IT DOES?

It is not rocket science.
There is no magic formula to planning. Data is collected, organised,
analysed and conclusions reached based on what has been found.
It's like a recipe of sorts.

Now we have had a closer look at what planning does, the next question is: How does planning do what it does?

The simple answer is: Planning does what it does by collecting data, making educated guesses and using human knowledge.

Collecting Data

Data is collected at the lowest possible level in a product's hierarchy; this is usually down to the size and colour level of the product hierarchy. That data is aggregated and presented as a summary.

The data summary is presented in the form of performance reports — standard and ad hoc ones — that get published across the business. This data is essential in understanding the performance of a business and knowing what is working and what isn't working.

These performance reports, especially the standard ones, highlight what is happening in the business and create discussion points for the weekly sales meeting.

Some of what happens as part of the weekly sales meeting is going through top sellers, bottom sellers, top sellers by brand, category supplier or any other grouping that fits the business.

Data is also categorised into formats that make sense. For instance, comparing this year's sales, stock and margin data to last years data for the same period. Being able to look at like for like performance, new business performance, promotional results and so on.

Like for like performance is when you compare the performance of what was around last year, usually stores, with the ones still around this year. So, using stores as an example, if there are new stores that opened this year, they would not be part of the like for like calculation as there were no sales in those stores last year.

Educated Guesses

Using a summarised form of data, planners are able to make educated guesses. For instance, say the same products consistently make the bottom 10 sellers week after week, physically getting samples of these products may show something to indicate why they are performing poorly. Such as, they may all be the same shade of a particular colour or a certain look may be a common factor in each of the bottom 10 products. The logical conclusion to come to would be that particular colour, shade or look does not resonate with customers. Doing this is particularly useful within fashion where there is a limited shelf life for items.

Once that conclusion has been reached, the next step a planner would take would be to limit the retailer's exposure to those products by trying to reduce inventory. This can be done in a variety of ways. Markdowns, returning stock to suppliers and cancelling future orders are a few ways inventory exposure can be reduced.

By looking at data and making educated guesses, planners come up with a set of recommendations, which is passed on to the decision makers.

Human Knowledge

Even though merchandise planning is a versatile role in that it is easy to move from one type of retailer to another, there are planners that opt to stick with a specific industry type, such as fashion. This is a personal decision made by individuals as to whether they would like to stick with one industry type or not.

Planners get to learn about the industry they are in and what its idiosyncrasies are. Yet, it is not uncommon to see planners work in a variety of industries throughout their working lives. It is neither an advantage nor disadvantage to hire planners with knowledge of multiple industries. As, at the end of the day, the role of a planner is to make as much profit as possible with the tools available.

As stated earlier, expertise in a particular product area is a secondary requirement to the skills needed to be successful within the role. So, the more experience gained as a planner within different retail industries the better, as it allows planners to make decisions based on what has happened or what they have seen happen in the past.

Product Planning Levels

All retail businesses, regardless of size, have a product hierarchy in place and it goes something like this.

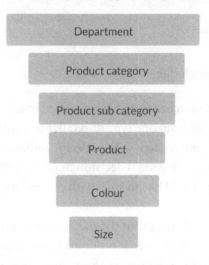

Example of a product hierarchy

When a planner is coming to grips with a new product area or retail industry, using these levels provides a starting place in becoming familiar with their new area of responsibility.

Along with the product hierarchy, there is also channel hierarchy, which is different for each business. An example of channel hierarchy for a brick and mortar store could be: Individual stores belong to an area and each area is part of a region and each region feeds into the national level of stores.

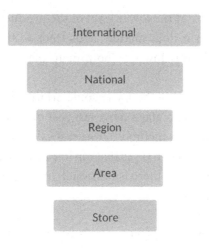

Example of a channel hierarchy

Channel hierarchy in an online pure play retailer, i.e. a retailer that is 100% online, would be similar; however, instead of looking at each store, we look at total sales from customers. A map can be used to group customers by geographical location or demographics can be used instead if that information is available.

No matter which method is used, the end result is the same. Data is collected by location and assigned to different levels of both the product and channel hierarchy.

A question to ask here is: Does the channel a customer uses to purchase a product affect how a planner plans?

There is no simple answer to this. It really does depend on what information is needed from a top line perspective. However, when you look at the lower level of the product and channel hierarchy, yes it does matter. This leads to the question of whether to do 'top down' or 'bottom up' planning.

Using a top down method, you could arbitrarily forecast sales to be a certain percentage above last year or even last week. Be mindful using this method to forecast sales, as upon a closer look at sales needed to get to that top line forecasted sales figure, it may turn out that there isn't enough inventory available for it to be achieved.

This is why, when budgeting or forecasting sales, it is always worthwhile to do 'top down' as well as 'bottom up' planning. If there is a gap between the two figures, then a decision needs to be made on whether the gap is to be closed, revised or left as is. No matter which number is used, everyone needs to agree on the figures to use.

Planning by channel would be handy here or at least viewing performance results by channel. This way you can tell which channel brings in the most profit and sales revenue. It also allows you to determine how much inventory to assign to each channel.

You see, when looking at things from a top line view, opportunities and potential issues do not get seen.

Also having channel information not only identifies where to house inventory if inventory is held by the retailer, it also identifies where to advertise products. That is to say, there is no point advertising a product to all customers if the product is only relevant to a select group of customers.

The channel with the largest increase in sales year on year and the main sales channel would be where a planner would concentrate their efforts.

Retail, Cost, Or Unit Planning

There are three units of measurement planners use when looking at performance. Each one has a purpose and is used in different ways. The three units of measurement are: Retail, cost and units.

Using retail values to measure performance is most commonly used when looking at sales, as opposed to reporting sales using cost or unit sales.

When looking at revenue, it is more often than not sales revenue that is quoted. Whether or not tax is deducted from the sales revenue figure is something that each retailer tends to decide for themselves. Generally speaking, I tend to verify for myself if tax is included in the sales revenue figures on reports I use. In doing this, I have found that some retailers record sales revenue with tax included and some with tax excluded.

As for inventory, some retailers report inventory figures based on retail value and others at cost value.

Each planner has a preference on what value they prefer working with for inventory, which may stem from how they were trained. My preference is to look at inventory at cost rather than retail. When people ask why I prefer looking at inventory at cost, I tell them it is because that is the value the inventory was purchased at; also there is no need to keep revaluing inventory whenever there is a price change or promotion. In other words, it is easier working with inventory at cost rather than at retail.

This does mean sales would need to be converted to a cost figure when doing any inventory calculations. This isn't an issue as cost of goods sold can easily be calculated and included in reports.

Sales at retail less tax and inventory at cost is my preference, as goods are paid for at cost and not at retail value. In other words, I prefer using the hybrid method of planning. There are pros and cons whether you plan at cost, retail or a combination of both.

Whether you plan at cost or retail, having to take into account markdowns is something that needs to be done. This is made easier to do with a hybrid planning method by using margin rate.

In all my years in planning, the hybrid method has been the most common method I have come across. As for planning in units, this is not something I have come across. Theoretically, there should be no reason sales and inventory can't be planned solely at the unit level. Realistically, it really doesn't make sense as margin value is not something that can be measured in units.

A good option is to have all three units of measure on planning documents. That way the most appropriate measure can be used. All that would be needed would be a big enough sheet of paper that would allow the document to be read easily when printed. For those who are able to read on screens, having the ability to view the document using different viewing options would be ideal.

NO PLANNING? NO PROBLEM

Planning as a function can be implemented in any sized retail organisation, all that's needed are processes to be set up and maintained.

If you started working for a retailer with no merchandise planning function, what would be the first thing you would do?

Other than finding out from senior management what information they would like to see, one of the first things to do is have a look at what information the retailer currently has and uses. Then the next step would be finding out where the information is stored and at what level it can be extracted.

The figures needed to compile any report are sales units and value, cost of goods sold value, inventory in units, cost and retail value.

These figures would be needed at different levels of the product and channel hierarchy. Also handy to have are cost price and selling price per unit.

This information can be used to get margin figures, SOH figures and answer questions like how long stock on hand will last.

That takes care of current data.

You'll also want to find out how long historical data is kept for. At the minimum, there should be the current year and the previous year's data on hand at all times. Data will be needed going back further than that, but as it is not needed on a regular basis, it is not essential to have it to hand at all times.

Personally, I prefer having easy access to the two most recent years of historical data and the current year's data to hand at all times.

So when you find yourself in a situation where there is no official planning department, the first thing to do is get data, both current and historical, get all current and future inventory commitments. The data collected can then be used to create a few standard reports that will give a simple view of current and historical sales, margin and inventory.

The other thing to do is ask if there is a sales and inventory budget and forecast in place. If there isn't, this would need to be created.

So, those are a few things a planner would need to do initially for a retailer who doesn't have an established merchandise planning department.

In order to get all this information, there would need to be collaboration between planning and whomever is the keeper of the information. Planners really do need to have good communication skills as the person or people who currently provide all this information may feel their role is being threatened by someone wanting information and questioning the accuracy of the information. This is human nature and thus, feelings need to be managed carefully. The last thing you would want is to spend time dealing with people issues before the department is set up. So, planners need to be thoughtful when requesting information.

Once familiarised with internal data sources, attention needs to turn to external data sources. How much inventory is yet to arrive? How much inventory do suppliers think the retailer has committed to? I like to check inventory commitments from suppliers as well as what the retailer thinks.

I also cross my fingers in the hope that the figures are the same. If not, then there is an issue that needs to be resolved. The ideal situation to be in is when there are no inventory commitment discrepancies to be resolved.

Once the standard reports are set up, budgets and forecasts created and inventory commitments identified, the planning department will not only be up and running, it would also be in a position to start communicating sales, margin and stock information to the rest of the business. As such, regular performance meetings can be scheduled in the calendar for all those who require the information.

Using this method is also a quick way to understand how the retailer operates and to become acquainted with the systems used. Chances are, though, that if a retailer doesn't have a planning department, a planner would need to use Excel to create reports. It may also be the case that current systems will need to be tweaked in order to get information more easily. This is an expense that a lot of retailers would rather not incur until a clear benefit can be seen from the introduction of merchandise planning as a function.

The skills needed by a planner aren't just to look at and understand numbers. An ability to liaise, communicate, investigate, collate, ask questions, analyse, deduce, decide and recommend are all skills needed in order to do the role. Could this be why planners move around a lot?

Also, would a retailer have a higher planner retention rate if all these skills are able to be used as and when needed? The thought here is, if the role a planner is hired to do doesn't make use of some or all of these skills from time to time, the planner will choose to leave in search of where these skills can be used and developed.

Another way to look at it is, if the planning role starts to narrow in its scope, there will be some planners who would find the environment one that doesn't allow them to flourish, resulting in them leaving.

As has been mentioned, the planning department should not be a standalone department. It is a department that needs to work with different areas of a business to perform its role well. Once data is gathered from multiple sources, it is collated and analysed. Before a decision can be made from the data, speaking to those who created the data, IT, customers, stores, logistics etc. may be required.

So, even though the main goal of a merchandise planner is to maximise a company's profits from sales, using minimal inventory, there is also a need for planners to understand retail and general business figures. Another skill to possess is knowing who to turn to in order to get answers to questions related to the accuracy of data.

This leads to a question that is often asked about planning. Is planning an art or a science?

We'll address this later on.

Outsourcing

There are a lot of business functions that can be outsourced. Social media management, copywriting, graphic design, marketing, accounting and customer service to name a few.

With this in mind, can an entire merchandise planning department be outsourced?

The easiest way to answer this question is to go through what a merchandise planning department does and if outsourcing would be practical.

Based on my definition of merchandise planning of *'...ensuring sales, stock and margin are aligned'*, we can start by looking to see how easy it would be to outsource these tasks.

Firstly, in order to align sales, stock and margin there needs to be some sort of plan in place.

Using a top down method, C level executives outline the direction to go in, the growth to strive for and the time period to achieve it in. With a bottom up method, data is collated and used to estimate what the sales would be for the planning period. A like for like sales lift or decline is added based on current sales trends, purchasing decisions and macro environment factors that directly influence sales, like an indirect tax increase or decrease, loss of a direct competitor, income tax increase or decrease etc.

The decisions made by C level executives can be partially outsourced by commissioning research. The company would research and prioritise what customers want. Once they have that information, they can then create an internal vision for the organisation.

The first couple of rounds of the budgeting process could be outsourced to an external organisation and then finalised internally.

As for inventory, the goal is always the same. To sell as much as possible off of as little inventory as possible without looking like you have run out of stock or have been left with too much stock. This area of inventory management could be outsourced, especially if whomever it is outsourced to has access to the sales target to be achieved. That way they can ensure there is enough stock to meet sales.

With the potential of sales and inventory plans being outsourced, it makes sense to also outsource coming up with a margin plan. After all, all three elements sit in the same document. The outsourced firm can recommend when to take markdowns, while ensuring the overall profit figure is met.

So, it is possible to outsource the task of creating a sales budget.

However, as all those who have created budgets know, as more information is made available, budgets get revised right up till the deadline. So the version submitted by the outsourced company would need to be adjustable within the organisation.

This creates issues in itself, particularly if the budget was created using a software package the retailer doesn't have access to. This could also make the cost of creating the budget much higher than if it was done internally.

Merchandise planning involves needing to make decisions on a day to day basis and reacting to sales quickly. If the whole function of a merchandise planning department is outsourced, it becomes difficult to make decisions quickly, potentially leading to lost sales or missing out on securing inventory.

Then there is the issue of information confidentiality. Accounting firms are used to dealing with multiple clients, sometimes in the same business space and they manage to keep all information about their clients confidential. Same goes for lawyers, although lawyers tend not to represent both sides in a case. Therefore, when outsourcing, there would need to be confidentiality rules in place to ensure information is not shared with competitors or anyone else other than the client.

This could be made easier by having a professional body for planners, like accountants. Although this may increase the cost of outsourcing and make having an in house planning department and planning system more cost effective. Particularly if the body requires its members to follow set guidelines

Ultimately, would you feel comfortable outsourcing your organisation's entire merchandise planning department?

Merchandise Planning Systems

Like any sort of system, there are different elements that go into it and a merchandise planning is no different. A merchandise planning system is one that pulls in information from various sources at different steps of a process, which then provides a complete view at specific points in time. The system would house historical, current and future information.

Such a complete system is usually created when a few systems integrate with each other, either directly or indirectly, via a third party.

A complete system would have information on things like: Sales, margin, cost of goods, inventory, purchases, location, product hierarchy (down to SKU), store hierarchy, supplier information, cost price, retail price and pack sizes. It would also have information on what actually happened, what the budget is, forecast, historical information and more.

Information is extracted using a reporting system. The system would have a standard suite of reports tailored to different parts of the business, including board level reports for upper management.

All systems would be managed by the IT department, who are the ones who make sure everything works the way it should.

The system is so comprehensive that planners are able to view sales of a particular size in a store at a specific time and date. From a planning perspective, the reason for this sort of granular information is so data can be sliced and diced in different ways when creating ad hoc reports.

For instance, say a supplier is out of stock of a popular product. Rather than the planner asking for information from various sources to calculate lost sales, the planner would be able to pull reports to see how much inventory is currently in the business, how long it would last, each store's average weekly sales and when the product would be back in stock. Even though the supplier may be able to electronically update when they are back in stock, it is still good to speak to them directly. A calculation can be done with this information to see how much sales would be missed and what the likely impact would be for sales and margin. If the product is seasonal, calculations can also be done to see if the entire stock on order is still needed or if it needs to be reduced.

Within a planning system, all this can be done in a short space of time, rather than across days if the planner has to source the information manually or from different systems that don't talk to each other.

The overall goal of any sort of planning system is to maximise return on investment. Whether the investment is in inventory, people or the system itself, the entire system needs to make decision making easier and faster. After all, retail is a fast paced industry and taking too long to make decisions can result in profit loss.

So, not only is it necessary for planners to liaise with other areas, planning systems also need to do the same thing.

Having a planning department and planning system shows no department stands on its own. The idea would be for the system to work seamlessly and integrate with each other at all business levels, i.e. from business decisions made in the boardroom, to coming up with an action plan, through to execution.

Board level decisions, which usually covers the medium to long term, get converted to metrics and indicators. These are then broken down into a stepped plan over time.

The stepped plan is used to create top down budgets and forecasts. At the same time, each department creates a bottom up budget. This is actually another requirement of a planning system: The ability to do top down as well as bottom up planning.

Merchandise planning systems need to be flexible enough to construct a budget using both the product and store hierarchy. The system also needs to be able to compare actuals with plans and needs to allow plans to become forecasts.

All this information can then be housed in a single system.

A merchandise planning system needs data to be entered at different entry points and extracted in similar ways. Purchases, allocations, sales, cost of goods etc, all need to be entered into the system or extracted from the system, based on the requirement of the user at different points in time.

I suppose when you think about it, a planning system is a way for things to be kept tidy, organised and in a central location that everyone can access easily in order to complete their jobs as efficiently and effectively as possible, with minimal hindrance from others.

For those worried about data security, there can be restrictions placed around who can access what data based on their role within the organisation.

PLANNING: ART OR SCIENCE?

Being subjectively objective!
Is planning art or science? This is a question with no
straightforward answer. All the numbers make it scientific, coming
up with recommendations and implementing them makes it an art.
So, perhaps it's a little of both...

As someone who steered clear of most science subjects at school, with the exception of Chemistry, which had more to do with curiosity for mixing things together to see what happens rather than what it could lead to, I subjectively lean towards planning being an art rather than a science.

Similarly, as I only passed the Financial Accounting module at university by the skin of my teeth and the Statistics module just confused me; it makes me believe planning is not a science.

Thankfully, I found the Management Accounting module at university a breeze and achieved very high marks. The Management Accounting module just made more sense to me. It also made me realise I am able to take qualitative data and convert it to quantitative data.

Knowing that numbers had narratives attached to them and that I was interested in the narrative, the numbers became a means to an end for me. It also meant that even though I saw planning as an art, there was a science (or logical foundation) to it as well.

Now, I think of planning as equal parts art and science. It's numbers based, which is the science part. How those numbers are interpreted and used is the art part. Whenever there is no data available to use, merchandise planning becomes an art form. As data becomes available, it becomes more of a science as there is evidence to back up what is being done.

Companies that see the planning function as being either art or science do not truly understand the planning function. Chances are they also see it as a standalone function, with the sole task of crunching numbers and one that only needs to be involved after products have been bought.

Thus, having a business brain in planning rather than an analytical brain may seem unnecessary to them; however, both types are needed.

Why equal parts science and art?

Well, science deals in facts and empirical proof. Statements are made and conclusions reached that can be backed up with data. It is absolute. Art on the other hand is abstract. It starts with an idea, a vision, a gut feeling that may not make sense, can't be proven and doesn't even seem likely based on information currently available.

Science deals with the searching and data gathering side of planning, reporting what has happened, analysing the data to communicate results and calculating likely outcomes using different scenarios.

The art side of planning comes into play when the information the data gives is used to improve performance. Coming up with action plans, tactics, strategies and goals to achieve are some examples. In other words, making connections between the data and the effect it has on customers.

This side of planning comes through in the form of recommendations planners give and ideas planners have, that are communicated to those who are in a position to make things happen.

Along with planners being scientific and artistic, having good communication skills is important in order to communicate findings or recommendations and speak about decisions made to company managers, external suppliers and colleagues. Computer literacy and proficiency in certain software packages (which can be learnt) forms another crucial component for planners to be successful.

So, when faced with the question: Is planning an art or a science? my answer would be both. There is a scientific element to it that is based on the calculations used. Once all the calculations are done, the artistic, abstraction part of planning comes into play.

TECHNOLOGY IN RETAIL: YESTERDAY, TODAY AND TOMORROW

Artificial intelligence and bots.
A subjective and somewhat extreme view on how technology could
affect merchandise planning in the future.

The world as we know it is changing at an alarming rate.

In my lifetime, there have been lots of changes, the biggest one being the world wide web. Prior to the Internet, getting information was a laborious process, which usually involved a trip to the research section of the library. Now, we have lots of answers literally at our fingertips, which means we also have a much shorter attention span and want instant answers to questions.

What is artificial intelligence, aka AI?

According to TechTarget[3], a site that brings together technical content, technology buyers and technology providers worldwide, artificial intelligence is: '...the stimulation of human intelligence processes by machines, especially computer systems. These processes include learning (the acquisition of information and rules for using the information), reasoning (using rules to reach approximate or definitive conclusions) and self-correction.'

Essentially, I see artificial intelligence as an attempt to, dare I say, create humans in a different form.

If successful, can AI do the role of planning in organisations?

How would artificial intelligence do this and more specifically, how would it fit into merchandise planning as we know it today? In other words, can a planning department be replaced

---

[3] **https://searchenterpriseai.techtarget.com/definition/AI-Artificial-Intelligence**

with bots?

As much as I would like to say no, I have to admit I can see a world where artificial intelligence can perform the role of a merchandise planner. Looking around now, there are certain tasks that are already being done with software that had been done by humans previously.

To illustrate just how much things have changed, let me tell you a story. My third ever role in retail was working on the shopfloor of a footwear company in the UK called Freeman, Hardy and Willis. Starting off, I worked four hours on a Saturday during the school term time and then I quickly became Saturday supervisor, which came with the added responsibility of organising breaks and assigning sections for staff to take responsibility over during the day. I was also responsible for closing the store at the end of the day, which involved counting the day's takings. Once I had reconciled the till, I had to place a phone call where I gave a voice on the other end of the phone what the day's takings were.

Today, there is no need for a phone call to be made unless all systems are down, as that is all dealt with electronically.

Another example is how stock is sent to stores. Before stock allocation software was around, stock was sent to stores manually. Calculations were done using comptometers and calculators. Figures were written on a sheet of paper, quantities were checked and messages sent to the warehouse. Now, systems do this role. Rather than checking each store's allocation manually, outliers are checked instead to ensure stock received can be sold by that store.

Calculating how much was available to spend on inventory in order to achieve sales was calculated manually. Now these calculations are done using software that integrates with other parts of the business.

So, it is safe to assume there are more and more planning tasks, particularly around the science side of planning, that will be done using artificial intelligence going forward. What does this mean for planners?

At a guess, it means there would be less of a need for planners as we have them today. The role won't go away completely, as new roles would be created and people would still be needed for the art (or interpretation) side of planning. It would just be given a different title, with modified tasks to perform.

A modified task could be one that creates and maintains the system and fixes issues that arise. These people would need to have knowledge about the science side of planning. The role could be called 'technical merchandise planners' or 'merchandise planning techs'.

Up until now, all technology used within planning has been dependant on humans getting the desired outcome by entering a set of parameters.

Technology is used to create purchase orders, send orders to suppliers and get orders delivered to stores. Technology is used to create budgets and forecasts. Technology is used to determine how long inventory is going to last. It is also used to collate sales information from multiple sources, such as stores.

All this is done with humans overseeing what the computerised system is doing. In other words, the orders are checked before being sent to suppliers. The quantity each store gets is checked. Budgets and forecasts are checked and tweaked multiple times based on external factors, ultimately at the direction of senior management and C level executives.

So, even though software attached to machines greatly help planners, at present, people are still needed to enter parameters each software uses in coming up with suggestions. People are also still needed to do the thinking and to sense check the figures generated by systems.

Could artificial intelligence remove the human element from all steps of the planning process? If this is possible and we fast forward into the future, would it look similar to this scenario below?

A request is made for an Artificial Intelligence Being (AIB), that will become an Artificial Intelligence Merchandise Planner (AIMP). Once delivery is taken for the AIB, teaching begins. The AIB is taught to gather information, process the information and summarise findings and then come up with proposals on a course of action to take.

The results from the course of action would be monitored and the AIMP would be able to use the results from whichever course of action taken to know how to deal with a similar situation in the future. In other words, the AIMP will learn from this experience and use it in future decision-making.

This is obviously a very simplistic view that is based on substituting how things are done today by people, with machines. The way in which the AIMP is taught to gather, process and summarise information makes merchandise planning more of a science than an art.

Even though the AIMP would be able to plan, forecast, budget, recommend, analyse and liaise with other AIBs within the organisation, one thing it would also need to do is factor in that part of human nature that gives us the ability to change our mind or come up with a solution that appears to be counter-intuitive because it is based on a gut feeling and not solely on quantitative analysis.

That is to say, any AIMP would need to factor in the art side of planning, which has a lot to do with why humans tend to have a change of heart.

Regardless of how artificial intelligence progresses, it is an area that will continue to affect merchandise planning in one form or another. Will it happen in my lifetime? Who knows!

Leonardo Da Vinci, Galileo, James Watt, Charles Babbage, Alexander Bell, Nikolai Tesla, Thomas Edison, the Wright Brothers and Tim Berners Lee are all people whose inventions are used in ways I am sure they never fully anticipated.

Personally, I see the art side of planning — which is also

called business interpretation or gut feel — to be where the competitive advantage lies for retailers and thus would like the art of merchandise planning to remain a constant part of the planning process. Although, a machine that is able to learn and think for itself does seem appealing.

There are so many questions with no answers when it comes to how AI will work. For instance, how long will it take for robots to become mainstream? Would AIBs be able to fix themselves when there is a glitch? Would there be a person overseeing them or will they oversee themselves? How would they get upgraded and how long would it take? Would it be possible to switch an AIB from say, working in a warehouse to working in the buying department? Would this be as simple as changing the 'brain' of the AIB or would the AIB need to be retrained in order to learn how to do the role? Most importantly of all, will AIBs be able to react to people's feelings and use this in making decisions?

These questions, while legitimate, are not ones that can be answered at present. We probably don't need to worry about them too much as AIBs haven't been fully developed as yet ...or have they?

For now, having a fully fledged AIMP is not on the list of potential uses of AI in retail. But the inclusion of AI in business is progressing. A 2019 IBM study, done in association with the National Retail Federation, surveyed 1,900 representatives in retail and consumer products in over 20 countries and identified the top six areas within retail where AI is planned to be used[4]. These are:

- Supply chain planning (85%)
- Demand forecasting (85%)
- Customer intelligence (79%)
- Marketing, advertising and campaign management (75%)
- Store operations (73%)
- Pricing and promotion (73%)

Even though 75 percent of respondents said they can see AI used in marketing, advertising and campaign management, I believe this is on the low side. Social platforms are increasingly becoming more automated. Posts can be scheduled in advance for days, weeks and months into the future. Scheduling software can determine the best times within each day to post, based on when your followers are most active.

There are even apps that create, schedule and then post images and links on social platforms after you've given the final approval. The app also refines its suggestions based on patterns it sees from approvals.

With this type of app already in existence and currently used, I see artificial intelligence within marketing, advertising and campaign management switching places with supply chain management as a top area in retail for AI would be used.

I can see this happening for a variety of reasons.

---

[4] **https://www.ibm.com/downloads/cas/NDE0G4LA**

Effect On Bottom Line

Marketing, advertising and campaign management are business costs where the returns received are not always as tangible as seeing stock being converted to sales.

Brand awareness does bring in sales; however, the cost of getting a brand name out there can be relatively high when measured against how much sales gets generated. Promoting specific products also increases sales of that product. Decisions on what to promote, which medium to use, how long to promote for and what the offer will be, can all be done using paid apps. These apps also let you analyse the metrics and other effects of each campaign.

It could also be argued that all digital marketing roles, especially the lower level roles, can and will be replaced with artificial intelligence. The reason being, these tireless AIBs will be able to create content, recommend courses of action based on pre-set parameters, execute promotions after the green light has been given and analyse and distribute results to other areas of the business, just like marketers do now. Managers will then be able to use all this in their planning and decision-making processes.

Yes, I can see artificial intelligence being effectively used in this area. It could even reduce the cost of acquiring new customers, while keeping the ones a business already has. It's likely that the cost of doing this will come in lower than in supply chain management as there are apps already doing or trying to do this. There are lots of different types of businesses out there to test the technology on, which also helps with costs, because all businesses, no matter the size, participate in marketing and promotions in one form or another.

My concern is, how far would humans go to get AIBs to perform tasks? At some point would we want them to take over the running of an organisation?

What's interesting is, supply chain planning and demand forecasting came in at the top of the survey list as the most likely areas in retail where artificial intelligence is planned to be used. These areas appear to be the most logical areas to start with and also the least disruptive, as they are already highly automated.

It would be interesting to know if artificial intelligence can be used to do roles that require decisions to be made with limited and incomplete information. Plus, what would be the cost of creating and deploying these AIBs? Who would foot the bill? These are worthwhile questions to ask as the cost could be prohibitive; thereby delaying things further.

Lots of questions, lots of opinions, lots of ideas. How will artificial intelligence be used in retail? How extensive will its use be?

We'll have to wait and see how it all pans out.

No Artificial Intelligence

Until AIMPs come into play and start performing the role of a merchandise planner, humans will continue to carry out the duties of a merchandise planner.

Yet, finding people to be merchandise planners is easier said than done, as different organisations have different ideas as to what a merchandise planner does. I often see job ads with a position title of 'merchandise planner' and as I read the tasks to be performed, it becomes clear the role is more about allocation than planning.

Then there is the difficulty of trying to find planners who are willing to put in the effort needed to get the job done. Other than the process-driven and predictable side of the role, which you could argue falls under the science part of planning, being a merchandise planner also requires outside the box thinking. This type of thinking usually happens outside of the normal working day and can result in innovative solutions to issues.

The current role involves liaising with other departments; talking to suppliers; dealing with internal and sometimes external customers; investigating why sales, stock and margin are not aligned and coming up with a way to realign them. With the amount of time needed, especially thinking time, to do some of these things, another question that comes to mind is whether or not planners always need to be in the office?

Merchandise planning is a role that uses a lot of grey matter to perform it well; time is spent thinking and deciding, based on audience: How best to present information, what recommendations to give, how to calculate the effect a certain campaign has had and if there can be some form of split testing done and coming up with a way to calculate the effect the additional revenue and margin will have if extrapolated.

That is to say, planners are always searching for things to implement to improve performance results.

Ways of Working

The way we work now is different to how we worked 20 years ago. There was a time when people were expected to do their jobs sat behind a desk in an office. Then some companies' modes of operation, people's lifestyle, along with technology, changed and it became possible to work from home on occasion. Now, some people are able to work remotely and some roles aren't restricted to being performed in an office. Face to face meetings can be conducted via video calls, presentation decks can be shared on screens during meetings and you can still send cheeky notes to each other in meetings using your preferred private messaging system.

In other words, the way we work is changing. Projecting forward, do you think a time will come when we'll be able to spend more time with friends and family than we do with colleagues?

There are some roles better suited to working remotely than others. Traditionally in retail, planning has been one of those roles that has been performed mainly in person, particularly when trade meetings take place. Having said that, people can dial into meetings if they are out of the office. From past experience, communicating over a speakerphone tends to slow down meetings as people tend to talk over each other. The reason being, there's no visual cues to know when people on the other end have something to say or have finished speaking.

As technology improves, there is nothing restricting the role of a merchandise planner being performed completely remotely. All data can be entered and extracted remotely, group calls can be done over video, screens can be shared, etc. In fact, with multiple people, video calls are much better than audio only calls, as it's easier to read facial expressions and cues when you can see someone talking.

Remote working benefits both employers and employees. Plus, it may become easier to get the type of merchandise planning professionals you actually want because working permit visas, sponsorships and interstate moves may no longer be needed.

Remote working is something employers need to embrace. It will likely move from being a side benefit to a requirement when deciding whether to apply for a job or not.

There are other aspects and benefits of being able to work remotely for both employers and employees. Employers can have smaller offices and have periodic face to face sessions, similar to a conference or kick-off. Employees, on the other hand, will need to have dedicated space in their homes to accommodate being able to work from home. There will need to be a reliable way to access, share and securely store data.

Access to reliable and fast Internet connection would also be needed.

A BRIEF HISTORY OF RETAILING: 1700 ONWARDS

Retail is here to stay!
Retail is not dead. It will never die. It has been around a long time and will continue to be around long after we are all gone. The same goes for the function of merchandise planning.

As mentioned earlier, retail has been around in one form or another for centuries. It wasn't until the turn of the 20th century that retail started to take the form we are currently used to seeing. Before 1900, there were only a few retailers that resembled the concept of retail we are used to seeing today.

Department stores, high streets, shopping malls, online stores all have one thing in common: Making things easier for customers. These methods of getting products into the hands of customers all allow customers to *'window shop'* without the pressure to buy.

Before then, department stores, some of which are still around today were exclusive places visited only by those in society who could afford the prices, those who worked there and those who made deliveries to the store.

Some of these stores are still operating today, albeit in a different format to how they first started.

Fortnum & Mason

Fortnum & Mason, also known as Fortnum's, first opened it doors in 1707 in London. Inauspiciously, it started in a spare room in Hugh Mason's house and is the oldest operating department store in the UK, if not the world.

Prior to the store opening, William Fortnum, who was a footman in Queen Anne's household (someone whose duties included admitting visitors and waiting at tables) dreamed up the idea of selling half used candle wax for a profit[5]. Hugh Mason already had a small store, so they combined their resources to create Fortnum & Mason. Hugh Mason had the customers and William Fortnum had a product to sell.

After profiting from half used candle wax and inventing the Scotch egg, Fortnum's provided groceries in its early days and is still known for food today. They have an extensive range of hampers, which they are well known for around the world. Along with food and hampers, you can also get cookware, fragrances, toiletries, clothing and yes, candles are still sold in the store.

Fortnum's serves a specific niche market that they have managed to hold onto since they first started trading. This doesn't mean they haven't evolved. It is the store's ability to evolve that has kept the doors open. Those who influence the direction the store should go in have been able to read the pulse of the market and react in a timely manner. This has been done while maintaining their core clientele base, who are those who have the funds to pay the high prices charged.

Sold in 1951 to W. Garfield Weston[6], the store still remains an iconic British establishment.

In terms of planning, at the beginning of Fortnum's there was no merchandising plan put in place. An opportunity was simply

---

[5] https://www.fortnumandmason.com/information/our-history

[6] https://www.telegraph.co.uk/finance/2809622/The-Weston-fortune.html

seized upon and exploited. Not knowing what went through the mind of Hugh Mason and William Fortnum when they started the store, one can only speculate their plan was to keep growing by being the first to introduce new things their client base would be willing to try and if they liked it, become repeat customers for that product. In other words, after testing the market with new products, they sold what worked and stopped selling products with no demand.

As for customer service, there would have been no browsing. You'd have had to know what you wanted before you went in. There would have been no exchange of cash, as invoices would have been sent at the end of a specified period for payment to be made. Afterall, discussing money, prices and exchanging cash was considered to be vulgar.

Le Bon Marché

Fast forward 130 years to 1838 and going across the channel from Fortnum and Mason and before Le Bon Marché[7] opened it doors, there was a novelty shop called Au Bon Marché[8]. Au Bon Marché was owned by Paul Videau and Aristide Boucicaut.

Aristide Boucicaut was born into retail as his father owned a small shop that sold items for a woman's wardrobe, like fabrics and ribbons. When he moved to Paris, he carried on working in women's clothing and went into partnership

---

[7] **http://www.globalblue.com/destinations/france/paris/history-of-le-bon-marche**

[8] **https://en.wikipedia.org/wiki/Le_Bon_Marché**

with Paul Videau, where, amongst other things, customers were allowed to browse and touch clothing before purchasing. He also introduced fixed prices, seasonal sales where prices were reduced on selected items and the concept of buying in bulk and selling for a lower margin. He also advertised in newspapers and drew people to the store through the use of window displays.

Boucicaut and Videau's partnership ended in 1851, with Videaus selling his share of the business to Boucicaut.

In 1852[9], Le Bon Marché opened its doors and is considered the first modern day department store.

Aristide Boucicaut ran the store the way he wanted. Boucicaut introduced reading rooms in his stores, which gave men a place to wait while women shopped; he introduced a mail order catalogue; prizes; entertainment for children and other ideas that increased sales exponentially over short periods of time. Le Bon Marché offered a shopping experience for its patrons that no one else was offering at the time in Paris, possible even the world.

For stock that didn't sell, he introduced seasonal sales to clear out excess inventory.

---

[9] https://www.lvmh.com/houses/selective-retailing/le-bon-marche

92

Macy's

Not long after Au Bon Marché become Le Bon Marché and across the Atlantic Ocean from Europe, a department store was opened in New York by Rowland Hussey Macy. Called R. H. Macy & Co[10]. Its doors opened in 1858.

Through advertising and associating itself with American traditions, Macy's has been serving customers all over America for over 160 years. In 1924 Macy's started sponsoring the New York Thanksgiving parade and in 1976 Macy's started sponsoring the 4th of July fireworks in New York. By sponsoring these events, Macy's has established itself not only to be a true American department store, it has also tied itself inextricably to the city of New York.

Selfridges

Fast forward to 1909 and back across the Atlantic, Harry Gordon Selfridge opened his store, named Selfridges[11], on the less fashionable end of Oxford Street. Unlike other stores in London at the time, customers were able to walk into the store simply to browse. Products were kept within reach of customers so they could not only browse, they could also touch before purchase.

Selfridges used similar tactics used by Aristide Boucicaut in the 19th century. The store was heavily advertised; excess and

---

[10] **https://www.macysinc.com/about/history**

[11] **https://en.wikipedia.org/wiki/Selfridges**

slow-moving inventory were cleared through using seasonal sales.

As part of Harry Selfridge's innovative approach to marketing, he also wanted to make sure anyone, regardless of budget, could walk into a store and buy something. As part of his marketing efforts to get the store well known across different socioeconomic groups, he, like Aristide Boucicaut, found ways to get people to come into and stay longer in the store by doing things like displaying the first aircraft that successfully flew across the English Channel in the store. Anyone could go to the store to look at it. There was no pressure to buy.

He also popularised the use of window design by having breathtaking designs that were kept lit all night. To this day, the Selfridges window displays are a destination in itself.

These department stores are still around today, not because of the products they sell or their location. They are around today because their founders refused to stop innovating. The founders were determined to keep moving forward, even after they had become successful. Even today, long after the founders have gone and ownership is no longer in the hands of the original families, these stores are still prospering.

Amazon

Started in 1994 selling books online, Amazon[12] currently is, amongst other things, an online retailer that sells a variety of products to its customers. Unlike other online retailers that specialise in just selling products, Amazon is a technology company that has specialised in getting goods and services to customers quickly.

As a technology company, having physical space has not been an issue and this has allowed Amazon to grow exponentially. Today, Amazon has an online department store, cloud storage services, a video streaming service, audio bookstore and music streaming service, with more services to come.

An online department store with thousands of products, Amazon has given anyone who wants to sell a product a platform to use. Along with this, Amazon keeps innovating by testing new ways to get products to consumers.

Always diversifying, Amazon is also showing an interest in brick and mortar retailing, rather than having a presence solely online. This further proves that there will always be a need and place for stores with a physical location in the world of retail.

Other Retailers

Other retailers of note that changed the retailing industry have done so by utilising a unique selling proposition that resonates

---

[12] **https://en.wikipedia.org/wiki/Amazon_(company)**

with their target customer and positions them firmly in the minds of other potential customers.

Retailing with a Conscience

Anita Roddick, founder of The Body Shop, was among the first to sell products in simple packaging, offer fragrance free refillable bottles and use ethically sourced ingredients that had not been tested on animals.

In essence, she used social and environmental issues to create campaigns that helped promote the business, which effectively started to make consumers think about where the products on the shelf originated from.

Conscience retailing, which is when retailers support specific causes, is now commonplace.

'Stack Them High, Sell It Cheap'

The phrase *stack them high, sell it cheap*, also seen as *pile it high, sell it cheap,* is one that has been attributed to Jack Cohen, the founder of Tesco.

The idea was that good profits can be made by selling large quantities of low priced, low margin items in a short space of time. This is done by benefiting from a higher rate of sale, i.e. stock turn, rather than selling small quantities of high priced, high margin items with low stock turns.

Other retailers that follow this method of retailing are Walmart and subscription based retailers, like Sam's Warehouse and Costco.

Fast Fashion

Speed is always an advantage in retail, which is why those retailers who can get new products onto the shop floor quickly so customers can purchase tend to capture and increase their market share.

Hennes & Mauritz, Mango, Zara, Topshop and Primark are retailers that offer fast fashion. Entire product lines are changed multiple times a season, rather than lasting the entire season.

Unlike the *stack them high, sell it cheap* approach, fast fashion uses the concept of make it fast, sell it faster. The principle of having a high stock turn also applies to fast fashion, as higher profit levels are achieved when stock is sold fast.

There is a common thread with all the retailers mentioned. That is, the founders focused on something special or unique that the store provided and used it to promote their store.

Fortnums created demand by focusing on half used candle wax from Queen Anne's household. The prestige attached to the wax, I would assume, allowed there to be an above average price charged, thus providing seed money for other ventures.

Le Bon Marché had a store that provided a shopping experience to its patrons with something to keep everyone entertained, making shopping an activity. Added to this, events, such as art shows, were also held in the store, which would have brought in a different set of potential customers.

Macy's attached itself to the city of New York by sponsoring two events in the city each year; thus linking the events and the store together. It also started the shopping experience before customers entered the store by providing a steam wagon to transport customers between its stores. This was because the flagship store, which opened in 1902, was located a fair distance from the original store.

Selfridges had its beautiful window displays, newspaper advertising, seasonal sales, different price points, an invitation to browse and so on, which all drew people into the store. These seasonal sales, browsing and different price points kept them in and got them to spend. They also had elevators for people to use to get between floors. That was a first for a London department store.

In summary, Amazon is all about speed of delivery to customers when a product is purchased online, The Body Shop is about offering guilt free shopping, 'stack them high, sell it cheap' is about not having customers miss out on products because there is none left and fast fashion is about feeding on people's fear of missing out.

Planning In Early Department Stores

How did planning work for the early department stores? Selecting products and ensuring there is enough inventory to meet the additional demand created by having seasonal sales, newspaper advertising and creating inviting window displays would have been the job of buyers not a planner. With no planning department, predicting the sales and profit to be achieved at a guess would have been done by an accountant or bookkeeper and may have been based on the amount of inventory they could get their hands on.

Today, sales decisions are not just based on the amount of inventory available. A planner also looks at what sales could be, then checks to see if there is enough inventory to meet the predicted sales. This process is done far enough in advance to ensure suppliers are able to make and deliver inventory on time.

In other words, centuries ago, sales levels were determined by what was available to sell. Today, amongst other factors, sales levels are determined by what the sales potential is and then getting inventory to meet those sales. The main sales limitations today comes down to maintaining and increasing the number of customers. By initially focusing on these areas, these retailers have shaped the retailing industry.

These areas of focus affect how merchandise planners create their plan, because a certain number of sales would come from these focus areas and have to be factored into sales, stock and margin figures. Proving again that planning is part science and part art, as marketing and promotion plans and the company philosophy get converted to figures and added to actual data to create a complete merchandising plan.

Integrating The Planning Function Into An Organisation's Culture

Since merchandise planning is not a standalone function in any retail organisation, the function is not as clear-cut as other functions within an organisation.

Most of the time, merchandise planning acts as a liaison between the corporate planning office and the buying office. Information is gathered, analysed and recommendations are made and presented.

Planning answers questions regarding future sales, margin and inventory levels. In order to have answers to these type of questions, planning deals with supply chain, allocation, purchasing, IT, stores, marketing and finance.

The information is deciphered and used to project gross margin, inventory goals and sales trends, as well as analyse sales, inventory flow and merchandise strategies. Using this data, the planning department prepares weekly and monthly reports that are published internally.

Along with attending regular meetings, planning representatives update forecasts using actual data and input from other departments and from management.

Even though buying and planning together form the buying department and work very closely together, they are separate functions. Buying is very much about giving customers the products they want and planning is about making sure there is enough inventory for customers when they want it, all while achieving sales and profit levels.

Both functions use past sales, usually collated by planning and market trend forecasts, usually supplied by buying as inputs to make decisions on what quantities to buy, how much to charge and where and when to stock them.

Planning also work closely with warehouses by providing them with projected sales volumes in units, so they can not only plan the flow of products in and out of the warehouse, they also get future visibility of when their throughput is expected to change significantly.

The warehouse have their own systems and can pull off historical data on when inventory came in and out of the warehouse. This information can be used to plan their activity levels. However, forecasting warehouse activity levels is made easier when everyone is working off the same set of figures. Thus, giving the warehouse an inventory budget and updated forecasts would go a long way towards ensuring there are no issues with the availability of inventory.

Sticking with inventory, planners, in conjunction with suppliers, also plan when purchases will be coming into the business. Knowing this not only helps the warehouse and stores, in the case of stock being sent directly from supplier to stores, it also helps planners know when money can be spent to purchase more inventory. In other words, having this information helps with open to buy management, which is the document used to ensure sales, stock and margin are aligned.

An example of planning working with other departments can be seen when proposing a promotional offer. Prior to the offer launch, planners use data to see if the promotion is required. This is done by deducing if the promotion is needed to increase sales or reduce inventory. Calculations are done to determine what the effect on margin would be during the offer period, the week, month, quarter, etc.

Planners would speak to the marketing department, who will create promotional materials and communicate the offer to all outlets to ensure all set-up is done prior to the promotion start date.

While this is going on, planners also look at inventory levels in stores. If stock needs to be moved around, planners instigate conversations that would take place between the logistics department, stores, as well as planning as to how stock can be moved between stores.

On top of all of this, forecasts need to be adjusted to show the expected results from the promotion and the effect it would have on overall sales, inventory and margin. Once all this has been done, the information is presented to senior management for approval, before it can be executed.

As you can see from this simple example, planning is not

a standalone department that just generates reports. The process to get an ad hoc promotional offer approved can be quite time consuming as it involves speaking to multiple departments. It also shows why there is a need to have some form of planning system in place, no matter how rudimentary, because identifying what type of promotion is needed, i.e. sales generating or inventory reduction, can be identified by monitoring performance before the need to have a promotion becomes very obvious.

WHAT DOES IT TAKE TO BECOME A PLANNER?

There is more than one way to become a planner.
There are many roads to use to become a planner. Each job
advertisement will have requirements for anyone who is looking to
apply for a planning role, ...but are all of them needed?

When planning roles are advertised, there are often three sections. There is a section about the company, one about the role and responsibilities of the position and one that outlines the skills the successful candidate will need to have. The list of skills acts as a filtering mechanism when going through applications received.

Most planning job vacancies include a requirement that applicants have some form of tertiary qualification, usually an undergraduate degree and have a certain number of years experience working as a planner. Other things listed as requirements for the role can include: results oriented, good interpersonal skills, ability to build and maintain relationships and the ability to work individually.

The skills and qualifications list is great and may cut down on the number of unqualified applicants received; however, in all my years as a planner, I've come to realise some of the things often listed are irrelevant when assessing if an applicant can do the job.

Undergraduate Degree

Having a tertiary qualification is not strictly needed to become a planner. It may be a regular requirement for the employer; however, it doesn't guarantee getting better quality candidates, especially as there are very few degrees around the globe where you can study merchandise planning.

I am lucky enough to have done a retailing degree and also work in retail. Although working in the field I studied in is more an exception to how things usually are as opposed to the norm.

The full title of the degree I have is BA (Hons) Marketing, Retailing and Distribution and it's from the University of Huddersfield. The title of the degree was so long it got shortened to BARD and that got reduced further to Retailing. So you see, I have always had to find ways to distil down what I am doing so it can be easily understood when people ask, 'what you do?'… or in this case 'what are you studying?'

After four years of study, which included a year of industry experience, I searched for and was offered a permanent role in a buying department. The retailer had a reputation for having an outstanding training program. It was at this point that I really started my training. It was a comprehensive training program that covered all aspects of the job I was hired to do.

Do I think having a university degree got me the job? No, I do not. It may have made it slightly easier for my application to get seen; however, observing the dozen or so people that were training with me, it seems having relevant experience would have also got my application seen.

Results Orientated

This role requirement is a bit misleading, since merchandise planners already know what results are required of them as they are all laid out in the merchandise plans, a.k.a. budgets that have been created. Plus, experienced planners know that once these plans are created, they are reforecasted when actual numbers start coming in. These plans get referred to when discussing what we wanted or said we would do in the budget. The reforecasting of the plan in effect becomes the new plan, which is referred to as the forecast and is the result being strived for.

Results Investigation

An additional skill criteria that should be added to skills needed by a merchandise planner is results investigation.

When things are going well, everyone is happy. However, there are two areas that a planner needs to excel at. The first is ensuring the season/year ends with inventory being in line with the budget/forecast and the second is having the ability to investigate and find out why things are not going well. That is to say, what is it that is driving both the good and bad performance results.

When sales and margin are down and inventory is up, merchandise planning is not a fun department to be in. It is during this period of time that tempers get frayed as questions are asked as to why things aren't going so well. When sales are down, there can be a lot of finger pointing and blame casting rather than working together to come up with a solution to turn the situation around. This is usually a sign of poor management from the leadership team.

It is also during these times that you may get some members of senior management or even the leadership team, coming to speak directly to planners as they themselves seek answers.

During this time, data becomes a place planners retreat to. The reason being data is often used to get a better understanding of why the results are the way they are, find problem areas, anomalies and test hypotheses.

Planners, along with buyers, also speak to those who are in the trenches, those who work on the shop floor, to get their take on sales performance, as they are the ones who deal directly with consumers.

Interpersonal Skills

If answers aren't definitively found in the numbers, the search continues by looking at other related areas and asking questions such as:

- Were deliveries into the business on time?
- Were stores sent inventory when they should have been?
- Did stores receive stock within the time period they should have?
- Did they get the quantities they were expecting?
- Was the stock received put onto the shopfloor as soon as it was received?

Once planners start looking at other areas of the business, it starts to cause friction between different departments, which is why merchandise planners need good interpersonal skills. In other words, planners need to play well with others. The last thing any organisation needs is lots of in-fighting as people start to defend their turf.

Calm Under Pressure

As mentioned earlier, when things aren't going well, all eyes are on planning as we are seen as data keepers. Needless to say, when there are questions or someone needs to know something, someone in planning is asked.

The person asking could be anyone. So, planners need to not only know how to stay calm under pressure when asked directly for data by senior management, a planner also needs to know how to manage the executive's expectations on how long it would take to get the information required. This is particularly true because the requests always seem to come when you have a lot on your plate.

Build And Maintain Relationships

This goes along with the interpersonal skills. Again, it is very easy to ruin a relationship between departments if planners demand information. As the saying goes, you catch more flies with honey than with vinegar. Inter-departmental relationships, once built, needs to be maintained so no one becomes defensive when sticky questions start being asked by planners. Questioning the processes used when you're investigating reasons for performance can raise hackles.

This skill is a tricky one as it involves having to read what communication style to use and what incentivises people. Added to this, when the person or people you have a relationship with move on from the department, new ones need to be formed with whomever takes over the role.

109

Work Individually

Nope, I do not think a requirement to be a planner is the ability to work individually or autonomously. This is because the planning department isn't a standalone department. The very nature of the role requires having to work with others.

Whether you use John Hobson's definition, my definition or the 5Rs definition of planning, planning must work with other departments.

Just getting sales information involves relating and liaising with the IT department or whichever department deals with the equipment used for transactions and the storage of transaction data. Planners also pass on the sales information to the accounts department, who use it to create their own monthly reports.

For stock, planning liaises with suppliers to ensure stock comes in on time; planning also liaises with the warehouse to ensure stock is sent out in the right quantities to the right stores and customers.

When it comes to margin, planners liaise with buyers on cost prices. Together with buyers they come up with a competitive selling price with good margins.

The need to work with others, such as the IT department, suppliers, accounts department and buyers, means planners rarely work individually.

Another key requirement of being a merchandise planner is

to be a self-starter. Specifically, this means being able to see an issue, investigate the cause of the issue and come up with a solution that works for everyone involved without losing site of what the issue to be resolved is.

Work Experience

Having experience is ideal, although when starting out in planning, chances are you'll have no experience.

When looking at job descriptions, the number of years experience mentioned is key in determining the type of role and also the level of pay. A role within planning that doesn't require any prior experience usually means it is an entry level position.

Up to two years' experience means it's a junior role, two to five years' experience means a mid level role and five or more years' experience means it's a senior role.

In my early days in planning, I worked within the fashion industry and one day I asked a recruiter how long I needed to stay in one role before moving on. I was told two years. This timeframe was selected because the first year was spent learning and the second year was spent utilising the experience and knowledge gained in the first year. This is a good rule of thumb to follow.

Good With Numbers

A planner doesn't need to be just good with numbers, we also need to be good at interpreting data by adding a narrative to it, translating qualitative data into quantitative data and deducing what will happen if certain actions are taken. Planners love scenarios.

Being good at maths isn't enough. This is why both quantitative and qualitative tests are sometimes requested as part of the recruitment process for planning roles.

Budgeting And Forecasting

If a person always likes being right, then planning is not a profession they should pursue and that is because planners are always wrong! The main thing to take note of is how wrong a planner is.

When creating forecasts, planners make a lot of assumptions. The assumptions are based on historical data, the direction C level executives have communicated the organisation is going in and effects of the political, environmental, social and technological terrain. Added to this, planners also look internally at an organisation and take into account its strengths, weaknesses, opportunities and threats. These are all factored in when coming up with budgets and forecasts.

Once actual numbers start coming in, it becomes clear that actuals are either better or worse than budgets and forecasts. Rarely, if ever, do forecasts represent the actual numbers reached. The closest I have ever got to having my forecast number match actuals was when I was about $10 under the forecasted number. Obviously, in percentage terms this would have been 100 percent accurate when rounded. Still, having the absolute number of a budget and forecast match exactly would be exciting.

Anyway, the point is, when it comes to budgeting and forecasting, planners are always wrong. Thankfully, it is the degree of inaccuracy that determines how good a planner is.

In other words, forecast accuracy is one measurement used to determine a planner's worth. Planners are more wrong than right in absolute terms, which is why measurements are looked at in a relative way. Percentage accuracy is the overall measure planners look to improve.

Forecast accuracy is important and is a metric used to measure how good a planner is. Of all the skills listed in job ads for planners, this is one that really measures a planner's worth. This is because forecasting things like sales and margin has a knock on effect in relation to how much can be spent in other parts of the business.

The calculations used to come up with a forecast is the science part of planning, which is done with software. Other ways software can be used to get a more accurate forecast is by getting marketing campaign data and overlaying that information onto the forecast figures as a way to improve accuracy.

If we lived in a world that had fully functioning Artificial

Intelligence Merchandise Planners (AIMP) that kept learning from data collected, there is no reason I can think of that would prevent an AIMP preparing budgets from start to finish and creating ongoing forecasts.

A Personal Thought on AI

My vision of artificial intelligence is not just the ones we see on TV and in movies, where they are human-like holograms. I see artificial intelligence as machines that can fit into objects. The object can be a computer, a watch, a TV, a robot and yes, a lifelike being. Ultimately, it will have a brain section that can be plugged in or unplugged.

Although, I have to say, as AIBs keep on learning, I also see them getting to the point where they are able to take over the world and humans become extinct.

Obviously, this thought stems from watching too many movies and TV programs and taking the idea of artificial intelligence to what could be seen as an illogical outcome. Then again we should keep in mind that as humans we are curious beings and we sometimes have tunnel vision and fail to fully think through the implications of our actions.

ABOUT ME

Who am I and how did I get into merchandise planning?

For the purposes of this book, I am someone who has been fortunate enough to have worked in a profession that directly relates to my field of study at university. This didn't happen intentionally. You could say it happened through a series of events that occurred over a period of years.

My very first job in England was being an Avon rep when I was 14. It was my first glimpse into the world of retail in the form of direct selling. It was a great gig as I was able to dictate my own hours; so it didn't interfere with my schoolwork, which in my family was my one and only priority. Due to us moving and me not having a mode of transportation to go to where my customers were, I quit that job and looked for another.

My second job as a teenager was working in a clothing store on the shop floor. The store had busy periods, but was mostly empty, so a lot of my time was spent sorting racks of clothes into style, size, colour order etc. When that got tedious, I quit that job. Quitting also coincided with taking exams, so the timing worked out well.

Having passed my GCSE exams at the age of 16 and started

college doing the A level subjects I wanted, I looked for another job. I initially got one in the food service industry, which I did not like and quit as quickly as I got it. I finally got a job in a shoe shop on the edge of central London. I did that job until I went on to university.

When I started applying to universities, I initially applied only to institutions that allowed me to do Business Studies with a major in Marketing. Carlisle University and Brighton University offered me places, subject to my A level grades. Fortunately or unfortunately, my A level grades were less than stellar. In fact, of all the exams I had done in my life, my A level grades were by far the worst grades I had ever received. For some reason though, I was not disappointed, as the grades I received were directly related to the effort I put into studying. Little hint: Do not put off studying for major exams till the night before.

Another thing I knew was that I was not going to take any exams again, even though I didn't get the grades I needed to go to the universities where I had been accepted. All I had to do to get into university was go through 'clearing', which was a list published in newspapers of all courses across all universities in the UK that were still accepting enrollments. Doing this meant I had to be open to studying a Business Studies adjacent course.

Going through the list, I chose to contact universities that offered Marketing related or Business Management degrees. On the list of these was a university that offered Marketing, Retailing and Distribution. I was working in retail, wanted to major in Marketing and as for distribution, oh well, familiarity with two out of three isn't too bad.

I ended up doing my degree in Marketing, Retailing and Distribution, which, as it turned out, was a really good decision. There was also the option to do a placement year with the degree, which was handy as I thought it would be a good way to get real life work experience to see if I was happy with the path I was taking.

Some of my most vivid memories from university included walking between lectures and feeling overwhelmed with all the group assignments I had to do. It was then I decided to start making lists to make sure everything that needed doing got done. It was also while I was at university that I found watching Formula One was an excellent way for me to unwind.

For me, Formula One was not about cars going around the circuit lap after lap. It was about the dedication the drivers had to have in order to get their seats and it was about how the entire team worked together harmoniously to get the car onto the track on race day. It was about how they transported all the kit from one track to another week after week for 7 months of the year. It was about the rules, the telemetry, the minds of the team leaders, the politics and everything else that happens behind the scenes. The race itself was secondary to this side of Formula One for me.

Made ten times more enjoyable was listening to Murray Walker, with his predictions and 'Murrayisms' who, together with Martin Brundle, were comical. I remember during one race Murray Walker finished talking and there was silence. After a while, Martin Brundle spoke and apologised it took him so long to speak as he was trying to figure out the definition of one of the words Murray Walker had just used. I found this funny, as I had also been trying to figure out what the same word meant.

For my work experience year, I couldn't decide what type of job I wanted to do. I knew my ideal situation would be to work abroad; I just had to find something that would fit into the criteria for a placement, so I was able to pass the year.

As chance would have it, one of my lecturers that semester was promoting working in Eastern Europe and said if anyone was interested to come and see him. I went to see him and before I knew it, I was on my way to Brno in the Czech Republic to work in a Chamber of Commerce for three months.

Working for the Brno Chamber of Commerce was really good. I didn't speak a word of Czech; thankfully, the accommodation provided by the local university was full of friendly international students who all had a base knowledge of English. As for those who I came into contact with who only spoke Czech, let's just say, I learnt very quickly how to say things in a form of Czech.

After a couple of months, I was shown a newspaper clipping, from a friend who was doing his placement year in Vienna, about a British couple who had a few stores in Prague. I contacted them speculatively, introduced myself as a student from the UK studying retail and offered my services, which was accepted.

118

During my time there, I created reports, conducted store visits and did stocktakes in the warehouse. My time in Prague was different to my time in Brno. In the short time I spent in Brno, I had established a social network, whereas in Prague, I knew no one and had to start again. Moving away from university accommodation didn't help either, when it came to building a social network. Luckily, I was able to meet a few people based all around the city who were in a similar position.

One day my boss and I were chatting and she asked what I would do after university. I mentioned I would more than likely look for a role in marketing and may also look at something in a buying department, but not buying. That was the fateful time when she said she could see me as a merchandise planner.

There you have it. That is how I ended up in merchandise planning.

Stepping Away from Planning

For the most part, I really liked merchandise planning. Starting off as a merchandising assistant for Marks and Spencer. The training I got there was second to none.

At that time in the UK, there were really only two approaches to training planners. There was the Marks and Spencer way and the Arcadia Group way.

Marks and Spencer had an obviously hierarchical system where if you wanted to progress away from being a merchandising assistant, you had to do something called 'boards.' On the other hand, you could come straight into the role of a merchandiser aka merchandise planner using a different route.

For the entry method I used, training took up to 18 months to complete and during that time the main goal, other than learning how to do the job, was to lose your 'in training' status.

The good thing about working for Marks and Spencer at the time was that the pay for that level of work was better than if you did the same role at another retailer.

Another good thing for me was that during my time there, I learnt not to place too much emphasis on job titles, as there were people who had the same job title as I did and were performing a completely different type of role to me, which they got rewarded for financially.

After leaving my first real buying department job, I moved companies and countries. After a few years I ended up working for the online retailing arm of Walmart, based just outside of San Francisco. This was another momentous occasion in my career, as I was able to learn the intricacies of planning. This was largely due to the planning director and how she stirred the department.

All the knowledge I had that was in fragments got pulled together into one place, more specifically into a single document, which was used to narrate current, past and future performance. I still use that document today and it is one of the first things I create in each job I have had since.

Places I worked after Walmart didn't provide as much joy as my time at Walmart or other companies prior. There were varying reasons for this, such as: Expectations were not aligned, the structure of the organisations moved from being flat to hierarchical, changes in management, etc. The final outcome was, the joy and fulfilment I used to have working in a planning role had gone. I've found that once that happens, it's best to find that joy somewhere else.

That was when I knew I needed a change!

ABOUT SLOPPYSUCCESS

When you hear the phrase 'SloppySuccess' do you immediately wonder why success would be sloppy? Do you think those two words should not be together?

Or, do you understand what it means?

Ask yourself these questions.

Whenever you have been truly successful at something, was your journey a smooth one? Did everything go according to plan?

Chances are it didn't and in fact it was a little bit '...sloppy'.

Another question. How does one succeed at something?

Answer: By making a start! It doesn't matter how small a start it is or where you start from, so long as a start is made.

This is exactly what SloppySuccess #makeastart is all about.

SLOPPYSCLASSES

SloppySuccess creates online classes that are short and to the point. Each class aims to explain retail concepts to makers and sellers, in a simple to understand way by giving easily relatable examples with step by step explanations.

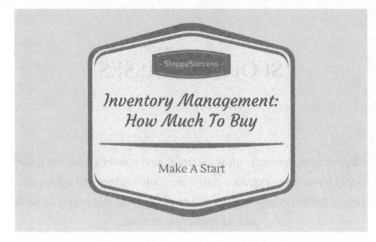

SloppySuccess

Inventory Management: How Much To Buy

Make A Start

How much inventory should I buy?

Class Description

Not having enough inventory or having too much inventory are two big issues retailers face. Why? Mainly because we are trying to predict the future in two ways:

1. What products people will buy; and
2. How long the product would be in demand

Answering these questions will allow you to calculate more accurately the optimal amount of inventory to buy.

This class has been created to guide you through a step by step process to use in calculating the optimal amount of stock to purchase for your retail business.

How do you decide what the best price to sell your product for?

Class Description

If you make and sell products or are thinking about selling products you have made, either online or in a brick and mortar store, knowing how to price your products is essential to the continued success of your store.

This class shows you how to come up with a profitable retail price to charge for your products that works for physical products you have made.

- SloppySuccess -

*Forecast Your Sales!
It's Worth It.*

Make A Start

Predicting the future.

Class Description

As Abraham Lincoln said, '*The best way to predict the future is to create it*'.

- Why not do this by creating a sales forecast.

I can hear the excuses going through your mind now.

- I am not good with numbers
- I do not need one for my business
- My accountant can do that

You are wrong!

No matter what type of business you are in — digital, product or service — you need a sales forecast. So, enjoy watching the class and learn how to put a simple forecast together.

More is not always better.

Class Description

This class aims to show you how to identify inventory you either no longer need or have too much of in your business.

We'll also go through what happens if you continue to sit on excess inventory.

There will also be tips given on how to get rid of excess inventory without crippling your finances.

Create your numbers plan.

Class Description

A class on creating a simple sales budget for my series on retail management concepts explained simply.

The purpose of a budget is to come up with an achievable plan that also sets expectations on how much you plan to make for the budgeting period.

This class aims to give an overview on how to create a simple sales budget primarily for physical products that can also be applied to digital or service products.

If you would like to see how adding returns to this budget would affect the margin value, go to www.sloppysuccess.com/returns-budget and fill in your details to receive access to the video.

A sales budget is a plan that tells you what direction to head in and acts as a reference document that sets sales expectations for a business.

This class can be watched in conjunction with my sales forecasting class.

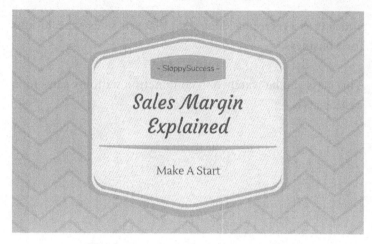

- SloppySuccess -

Sales Margin Explained

Make A Start

The first step in understanding profits.

Class Description

If you sell anything, you'll want to know how much profit, also known as margin, you have made.

This class aims to provide a basic explanation to help you understand how to calculate what your margin is.

It doesn't stop there though, as I also take you through the effect of what will happen if one element of the margin calculation is changed and why it is good to know what your margin rate is along with your margin value.

This class is aimed at those who buy and sell products or make their own products to sell and struggle with how to calculate margin.

If you can measure it, you can improve it.

Class Description

It always seems as if there are a million and one things to do when running a business, especially if you are the only person in the business.

The only way to combat this is to set yourself a business objective and work towards achieving the objective. By making sure the business objective is measurable, you would be in a position to narrow down where to focus your energy and proactively resolve any potential problems before they arise.

The key to doing this is to identify a few performance metrics that will get you the outcome you want and that is what this class helps with.

This class helps you navigate performance data to come up with the key data you would need to monitor current performance at a glance and identify areas that can be improved in order to improve overall performance.

Watch this class if you make or buy physical or digital products to sell to consumers. Although no prior knowledge is needed to identify areas to focus on, one thing you will need to know is what your business objective is.

You will also need data about your business so targets to achieve can be set and a summary table created.

MASTERING A NEW SKILL

A POST FROM SLOPPYSUCCESS' BLOG

The SloppySuccess blog contains a mishmash of topics and themes exploring concepts and ideas related to business, personal growth and life.

* * *

It Takes Time

How do we get good at anything?

The answer – by repetition and practise.

It is said that it takes 10,000 hours to master a skill. If this is the case, it would take working on something for 250 weeks, that is just under 5 years to master a new skill, assuming the skill is worked on for 8 hours a day, 5 days a week.

That seems like a long time to master a skill; after all, who spends all day doing one thing, day in and day out?

Studying

Professions leading to becoming doctors, dentists, lawyers, architects and engineers take a lot of time. This is because for these career paths, there is the theoretical as well as the practical part of studying that takes years to complete. Added to this, there are additional specialisations, which requires even further study.

This is why those in these types of professions never seem to stop studying.

Does this mean they are masters of their chosen specialty?

If they had less than 5 years' practical experience, then I would say they are well on the way of becoming masters in their field. If they have 10 or more years of practical experience, then I would say they are definitely masters in their field.

It is the practical experience that solidifies the knowledge. Being able to recall a previous occasion you have come up against a similar situation or being able to come up with a solution by applying your professional knowledge to a given work-related challenge shows you have mastered a skill.

Mastering A New Skill Is Scary

Making major life changes can be daunting.

Opting to change careers, having already become a master in your current field is scary.

Even going from being an employee to a business owner is scary as there is plenty of uncertainty when you own a business. The thought of having to start again from the bottom and work your way up is something not everyone is willing to do.

Losing or giving up the comfort and certainty you currently have takes a lot of willpower, which is why starting something new with no guarantee of success takes a lot of courage, determination and faith in yourself.

Summary

If you decide to change paths later in life that requires having to master a new skill, there will be plenty of people who doubt your ability to make the change.

By all means hear what they have to say; however, try not to let their words make you doubt your decisions.

Life is too short for regrets and fear is the only thing that would stop you from not changing paths later in life.

So make a start and begin mastering a new skill. Don't give up. Ignore those who don't believe you can do it and in time you will master your new skill.

GLOSSARY

AI: Artificial Intelligence

AIB: Artificial Intelligence Being

AIMP: Artificial Intelligence Merchandise Planner

Cost of goods: Total value of goods at cost. This could be sold goods or stock currently on hand

Cost price: The amount you are charged by a supplier for goods or the amount it cost to produce what you've made. This is usually quoted per unit, but can also be quoted for a pack

Cost price rebate: Discount given on the cost price of products based on an agreement between retailer and supplier

Demand: Popularity of a product which will translate to future sales

Inventory: Also referred to as stock, these are the products you have or are in the process of purchasing or that you own

Inventory budget: This shows the amount of inventory to send to customers, e.g. physical stores and how much inventory will be received for each month

Lost sales: Sales that did not materialise because of things like being out of stock, shop shut or site goes down during trading hours etc.

Margin: This is the difference between how much a product is sold for, less any taxes and the cost price

Order cycle: How often orders are placed

Order lag: The time difference between when order quantity has been calculated and when the order actually gets placed

Outliers: Results that fall outside the normal or expected range

Sales forecast: Prediction of how much would be sold over a specified period

Safety stock: Amount of extra stock to always have on hand in case there is a sales spike or delay in stock delivery

Stock on hand: How much stock is currently available and can be accessed

Units: Number of pieces

Made in the USA
Monee, IL
14 June 2024

59874154R00085